Finally—a short, simple book p
develop a lifestyle of biblical spi
stance or resorting to mysticism, legalism, or license. *Simplify Your Spiritual Life* fills a major void. If you practice even half of what Don Whitney recommends, your spiritual life will improve. Give this book a quick read, then go back and carefully read one chapter each day, pray over it, and implement it.

— Dr. Joel R. Beeke, president, Puritan Reformed Theological Seminary; pastor, Heritage Reformed Congregation of Grand Rapids, Michigan

Don Whitney has done it again! This book addresses the greatest fears about the spiritual disciplines—how can I practice disciplines without making it too complicated? *Simplify Your Spiritual Life* is the right message for the right time.

— Pastor Tedd Tripp, pastor, author, conference speaker

Whitney has done it again! *Simplify Your Spiritual Life* is a marvelous tool for repairing the foundations of your life by going back to study the basics of genuine spirituality such as the Triune God, Christ, Scripture, biblical meditation, and prayer. Though quickly read, each of the sections in this book can help you to know what you long for in the depths of your being—soul refreshment and the 'simplicity and purity of devotion to Christ.'

— Dr. Michael A.G. Haykin, professor of historical theology and reformed spirituality, Toronto Baptist Seminary, Toronto; adjunct professor of church history, Southern Baptist Theological Seminary, Louisville, Kentucky

The writing of Donald Whitney has been a tremendous source of strength and encouragement, both for me personally and for the church I have the privilege of serving. Here is a man who makes Scriptural truth clear and accessible to the ordinary Christian. This book will have a similar effect, not only simplifying your spiritual life, but deepening your spiritual life as well.

— CJ Mahaney, senior pastor, Covenant Life Church, Gaithersburg, Maryland

In these fast-paced times, most people feel too overwhelmed and overworked to spend very much time with God. But in this biblical, practical, and best of all, simple, book, Don Whitney gives dozens of helpful suggestions for cutting through all the clutter in ways that will help us grow in Christ. Most of us know we need to simplify; this wonderful book shows us how.

—DR. PHILIP GRAHAM RYKEN, senior minister, Tenth Presbyterian Church, Philadelphia; author of *The Message of Salvation*

Donald Whitney is a master teacher in the area of spiritual disciplines. And it is obvious that he writes from experience—he practices what he preaches. *Simplify Your Spiritual Life* will be helpful to both new and mature belivers.

—JERRY BRIDGES, author of *The Pursuit of Holiness*

This is a much-needed and wisdom-filled book. In our complex and frantic world, there is a crying need to simplify and prioritize, to move from trivial busyness to significant labor, to move from superficial contact to real fellowship. Don Whitney is your sure-footed guide from the "second things" to the "first things." His timely, biblical and practical advice and counsel will do many an overtaxed and frazzled soul spiritual good. Take, read, learn and grow!

—Ligon Duncan, senior minister, First Presbyterian Church, Jackson, Mississippi

SIMPLIFY YOUR SPIRITUAL LIFE

SPIRITUAL DISCIPLINES FOR THE OVERWHELMED

Donald S. Whitney

NAVPRESS®

BRINGING TRUTH TO LIFE

OUR GUARANTEE TO YOU

We believe so strongly in the message of our books that we are making this quality guarantee to you. If for any reason you are disappointed with the content of this book, return the title page to us with your name and address and we will refund to you the list price of the book. To help us serve you better, please briefly describe why you were disappointed. Mail your refund request to: NavPress, P.O. Box 35002, Colorado Springs, CO 80935.

The Navigators is an international Christian organization. Our mission is to reach, disciple, and equip people to know Christ and to make Him known through successive generations. We envision multitudes of diverse people in the United States and every other nation who have a passionate love for Christ, live a lifestyle of sharing Christ's love, and multiply spiritual laborers among those without Christ.

NavPress is the publishing ministry of The Navigators. NavPress publications help believers learn biblical truth and apply what they learn to their lives and ministries. Our mission is to stimulate spiritual formation among our readers.

ISBN 1-57683-345-3

Cover design by Ray Moore
Creative Team: Nanci McAlister, Greg Clouse, Amy Spencer, Laura Spray, Pat Miller

Some of the anecdotal illustrations in this book are true to life and are included with the permission of the persons involved. All other illustrations are composites of real situations, and any resemblance to people living or dead is coincidental.

Unless otherwise identified, all Scripture quotations in this publication are taken from the *New King James Version* (NKJV). Copyright © 1982 by Thomas Nelson, Inc. Used by permission. All rights reserved. Other versions used include HOLY BIBLE: NEW INTERNATIONAL VERSION® (NIV®). Copyright © 1973, 1978, 1984 by International Bible Society. Used by permission of Zondervan Publishing House. All rights reserved; and the *New American Standard Bible* (NASB), © The Lockman Foundation 1960, 1962, 1963, 1968, 1971, 1972, 1973, 1975, 1977.

Whitney, Donald S.
  Simplify your spiritual life : spiritual disciplines for the
overwhelmed / Donald S. Whitney.
     p. cm.
Includes bibliographical references.
  ISBN 1-57683-345-3
  1. Spiritual life--Christianity. 2. Simplicity--Religious
aspects--Christianity. I. Title.
  BV4647.S48W49 2003
  248.4--dc21
                                    2003002394

Printed in the United States of America

  4 5 6 7 8 9 10 / 08 07 06

FOR A FREE CATALOG OF
NAVPRESS BOOKS & BIBLE STUDIES,
CALL 1-800-366-7788 (USA)
OR 1-800-839-4769 (CANADA)

CONTENTS

For my descendants,
physical and spiritual,
present and future.

"This will be written for the generation to come,
That a people yet to be created may praise the LORD."
Psalm 102:18

FOREWORD

Do more and more with less and less—and do it faster and faster. This is the oft-heard management strategy in our profusely overloaded age. But what would Jesus think? Can you imagine Him flying past the blind beggar, sweat dripping off His brow, yelling at His lagging disciples because they were twenty minutes late for the Jericho prayer breakfast? How would He respond if cell phones went off within the assembled crowds at the Sermon on the Mount? Jesus had little tolerance for clutter or complexity. Simply put, He would not be distracted from His mission.

Jesus loved people and He loved truth. There was an unyielding simplicity about His approach, yet the result was freeing rather than onerous. His simplicity was all about focus. "One thing is needful . . ." are the words we remember.

Jesus practiced disciplines like solitude, prayer, and Sabbath because He sought the things above rather than the unfocused distractions of the world He came to save. And even though He was disciplined and focused, He was winsome to those with spiritual need. He served. He healed. He taught. He showed compassion. People saw, and responded to His simple message.

"Every age has its own characteristics," wrote pastor and author A. W. Tozer. "Right now we are in an age of religious complexity. The simplicity which is in Christ is rarely found among us." Against this problem, *Simplify Your Spiritual Life* confronts the clutter, complexities, and distractions of our age and brings us back to the simplicity of the kingdom of God. Don Whitney first bulldozes the often jumbled landscape of our spiritual condition and then presents Jesus before us front and center.

This book is not about an unsustainable perfection or an oppressive legalism but instead about the kind of simple devotion that sets us free. It is about the practical day-to-day of the Christian devotional walk, lived in such a way that intimacy with Christ can shine through. It is a much welcomed book about intentional living and the rediscovery of disciplines that have skipped generations but now are dusted off and brought back into the light for such a muddled time as this.

Richard A. Swenson, M.D.

Author of *Margin* and *The Overload Syndrome*

ACKNOWLEDGMENTS

*"First, I thank my God through Jesus Christ
for you all . . ." (Romans 1:8)*

Heartfelt thanks to . . .

- Caffy and Laurelen for your longsuffering, patience, and support in the completion of this book. I love you.
- Those who prayed for me. I received more assurances of prayer during this project than with anything else I've written. The Lord answered.
- Mindy Rose for all your practical help, which you always do so well and willingly.
- Nanci McAlister for your encouragement and support from the very beginning of this project.
- Susan Verstraete for your unselfish ministry with www.SpiritualDisciplines.org and in particular your help in promoting the book there.
- Amy Spencer for your diligence with details.
- Greg Clouse for your concern for the author as well as for the book.
- The many others who deserve appreciation for their contributions to this book.

"For God is not unjust to forget your work and labor of love which you have shown toward His name, in that you have ministered to the saints, and do minister" (Hebrews 6:10).

INTRODUCTION

The world is more complex than ever, and it becomes more so by the nanosecond. As a result, almost everyone eventually feels the need to simplify. For many people, simplifying means nothing more than "doing less." But simplifying is not so much about doing fewer things as it is about doing the *right* things.

This distinction is even more important when it comes to simplifying the spiritual part of life. For even the "ideal" simple spiritual life (whatever that is) will still be a busy one. Like Jesus and the apostle Paul, anyone devoted to loving God and people will lead a full and active life. But such a life will also be more focused, fruitful, and satisfying because it emphasizes the right priorities. So, while this book does have much to say about doing less, it says more about doing the right things, and doing them with the right motive.

Moreover, *Simplify Your Spiritual Life* is not, strictly speaking, a philosophy or theology of simplifying. While some of that is here, presenting the arguments for simplifying isn't the primary purpose of this book. These brief chapters are for people already convinced of their need to simplify where they can. In particular, this book is for those who want hope and help to start simplifying their *spiritual* lives.

I do not want to give the impression that I think everyone should do everything suggested in these pages. To do that would almost certainly result in further *complicating* your life. Rather, here is a field of ideas in which you can mentally meander, stopping to pick only those that will simplify your spiritual life.

As anyone who knows me well can testify, I write not as an expert, but as a fellow struggler in the need to simplify. Much of what's here has been forged by necessity as I've attempted to keep from being crushed by the weight of my own sense of overload. May the Lord use the fruit of this effort to refresh and strengthen your soul, and to keep you in "the simplicity and purity of devotion to Christ" (2 Corinthians 11:3, NASB).

SIMPLIFYING
AND
FIRST
PRINCIPLES

Simplify Your Spiritual Life

Does your spiritual life sometimes seem more like a burden than a blessing? Does your spirituality seem to exhaust you as often as it refreshes you? Have your spiritual practices become "just another thing to do" in an already overcrowded, stress-filled schedule? If so, then you need to simplify your spiritual life.

We should expect part of true spirituality to exhaust us, for it exists not merely for our own edification, but to serve the glory and purposes of God. Jesus' spiritual labors occasionally so fatigued Him that He could remain asleep in an open boat in the middle of a lake during a life-threatening storm (see Luke 8:22-25). Likewise, the apostle Paul knew the depletion of inner resources that results from the willingness to "spend and be spent" for the sake of the souls of others (2 Corinthians 12:15). All aspects of externalized spirituality—serving people's needs, doing good works, taking the gospel to the spiritually lost, working in church ministries—expend the reserves of both body and soul.

There's a problem, though, when the inflow of spiritual renewal doesn't replenish the outflow of spiritual ministry. Our spiritual life should be *the* source of inner *re*creation and restoration because it is the way we most directly experience the Lord Himself in daily life. Through our spiritual disciplines (rightly motivated and practiced) come many of the most refreshing blessings of knowing Christ.

An example of how the spiritual disciplines can be an ongoing means of reinvigorating the soul is depicted in Psalm 1:2-3. Frequent meditation on (and not just reading of) God's Word so continually refreshes the meditator that "he shall be like a tree planted by the rivers of water, that brings forth its fruit in its season, whose leaf also shall not wither; and whatever he does shall prosper."

However, as everything else in our lives becomes more complex, so can our spirituality. As one writer observed, "The pattern of over-involvement, clutter, and busyness that is a part of our lives at home and at work will follow us into our spiritual lives unless we are vigilant."[1] With increasing prosperity and technology come increasing opportunities and options—even in our spiritual practices—that weren't available a short time ago. For instance, instead of simply sitting in a comfortable chair by a sunny window with our Bible, journal, and pen, now we can

- receive devotional readings sent daily by automatic email.
- read the Bible in several of the many translations we possess, including those on our computer.
- make journal entries on the computer by keyboard or voice-recognition software, inserting interesting graphics along with the text.
- develop our devotional experience with worship-enhancing audio and/or video.

But it all needs to be done faster than ever before because of the strangling demands on our time.

The growing frustrations of hurry and complexity affect the practice not only of our personal spiritual disciplines, but also of our congregational spiritual disciplines (the ones we practice with other Christians). There's less time for church involvement than previously, and yet there are more church activities to choose from. We're so far behind in so many things that sometimes we wonder if what we receive from church is worth the overwhelming effort just to get there.

In some ways we're doing more than ever spiritually, but enjoying and profiting from it less. Many areas of our lives are productive and prosperous, yet we've never felt so spiritually withered. Our calendars are full, but our souls are empty.

The time has come to evaluate whether what we are doing in our spiritual lives is taking us where we want to go. There is hope. Read on.

VERIFY BEFORE YOU SIMPLIFY

THE PLACE TO START SIMPLIFYING THE SPIRITUAL LIFE IS TO MAKE SURE you have one.

Jesus frequently challenged the spiritual presumptions of His hearers. He did this constantly with an influential group of men known as the Pharisees. Because of the unusual depth of their interest in and commitment to the things of God (especially Bible study and memorization, prayer, and fasting), they and everyone else were sure that if anyone was right with God, it was these dedicated Pharisees. Jesus once devoted an entire parable to warn against the danger of the spiritual presumption of the Pharisees and people like them (see Luke 18:9-14).

The apostle Paul—who was once a Pharisee himself—likewise warned people about assuming that everything was okay between themselves and God. It was to a group of people who had shown great zeal as followers of Jesus that he wrote, "Examine yourselves as to whether you are in the faith. Test yourselves" (2 Corinthians 13:5).

Paul once wrote the following to a group of people he himself believed to have spiritual life: "And you He made alive, who were dead in trespasses and sins" (Ephesians 2:1). While physically alive, they had been spiritually dead. But, thanks be to God, "He made alive" by grace through faith in Jesus those who had been spiritually dead. When these people were spiritually dead, they probably thought they were spiritually alive. They would have imagined that they could have gotten as much out of the practices of Christian spirituality as anyone—provided they had any interest in them. And isn't that what most people think today?

However, the Bible says that until a person is given the Holy Spirit, he "does not receive the things of the Spirit of God, for they are foolishness to him" (1 Corinthians 2:14). No one has spiritual life who does not have the Spirit of God. And only those who know Jesus Christ through repentance and faith have the Spirit of God.

So the reason some feel frustrated about their spirituality is because they're assuming life and health when in actuality they're spiritual corpses. Upon what do you base *your* assurance that the Holy Spirit dwells in you and that you have eternal spiritual life? Do you know the biblical marks of the presence of the Holy Spirit (as in John 16:8-10,14 and Galatians 5:22-23) and the signs of God-given spiritual life (as in the letter of 1 John)? Can you see these in your life?

Be sure to verify your spiritual life before you try to simplify it.

Know the Good News
of Christian Spirituality

Not only have most people on the planet never heard the good news of Christian spirituality, I am doubtful whether many churchgoers have even heard it clearly presented. And some who have heard it thousands of times are tentative when asked about it.

Christian spirituality begins with one of the most important words in the Bible. That word is *gospel,* which is the English translation of the New Testament Greek word that literally means "good news." But as essential as the gospel is to Christianity, I have often encountered an embarrassing silence whenever I have asked church groups, "What is the gospel?"

Let me ask you. Suppose you were going to write the gospel in a paragraph or so and send it to a friend in an email or letter. Could you do it? Confidently? Why would it be "good news"?

One of the places where the Bible summarizes the gospel is in 1 Corinthians 15:1-8. The heart of this passage tells us that "Christ died for our sins according to the Scriptures, and that He was buried, and that He rose again the third day according to the Scriptures" (verses 3-4). So the gospel that produces genuine Christian spirituality is that Jesus Christ died, taking the guilt of sinners and the wrath of God upon Himself, and was raised bodily from the dead to show that the Father accepted His death for others and removed their sins. Christ's substitutionary death for sinners is the measure of His love, and His resurrection from the dead is the stunning confirmation that all He said and did is true.

This is good news—the *best possible* news—because it demonstrates, among so many other things, the willingness of the God we had sinned against countless times to draw us to Himself, to engage in an intimate relationship with us. It means that He has done in Christ what we couldn't have done for ourselves, opening the door for us to come in faith and to experience all the indescribable riches of fellowship with God, and thereby become "partakers of the divine nature" (2 Peter 1:4).

Do you know—by experience—this good news?

Rest Your Soul in "the Simplicity and Purity of Devotion to Christ"

In the early morning dim of March 29, 1849, a sympathetic storekeeper in Richmond, Virginia, nailed the lid on a crate containing a slave. A two-hundred-pound man had folded himself into a wooden box just three-foot-one-inch long, two feet wide, and two-and-a-half feet deep. Cramped in suffocating darkness, the slave endured—often upside down—a grueling three-hundred-and-fifty-mile shipment via railroad freight car, steamboat, and wagon. Twenty-seven hours later in a Philadelphia abolitionist's office, Henry "Box" Brown emerged from his coffin-like confinement to begin life as a free man. The news of his stunning appearance encouraged the hopes of freedom in countless slaves.

Everyone is born a slave of sin. Jesus Christ said, "Most assuredly, I say to you, whoever commits sin is a slave of sin" (John 8:34). We cannot free ourselves from this oppressive master, for no one can live without sinning against God. But the sinless Jesus—not for His own sake, but for others—came from Heaven to deliver His people. Jesus allowed godless men to nail Him to a Roman cross and three days later rose from the dead so that "we should no longer be slaves of sin" (Romans 6:6). And all those who trust in His work (and not their own) as the way to freedom will find emancipation from sin. "Therefore," declared Jesus, "if the Son makes you free, you shall be free indeed" (John 8:36).

I wonder if Henry Brown ever suffered nightmares of being back in his box? I do know that Christians—though freed from the penalty of all sin and declared righteous in God's sight—sometimes feel a spiritual claustrophobia. It's almost as though they've returned to the bondage that enslaved them before they knew Jesus. Sinful choices and activities can cause God's forgiven people to feel this way. But there are other reasons why believers may not be breathing the sweet air of spiritual freedom.

If you feel boxed-in spiritually, perhaps it's because you've experienced what the apostle Paul feared for the souls of some: "But I am afraid, lest as the serpent deceived Eve by his craftiness, your minds should be led astray from the simplicity and purity of devotion to Christ" (2 Corinthians 11:3, NASB). Paul's readers had been distracted by the message of "another Jesus" (verse 4). In other words, men had come preaching about Jesus, but spoke of Him differently than the apostle Paul had. Many think that false teachers had told them about Christ in a way that caused them to look less to Jesus and more to their own good deeds and spirituality. As they did so, they were "led astray from the simplicity and purity of devotion to Christ."

Whenever this happens to a Christian, his spiritual life soon becomes burdensome. He feels "back in the box" of slavery to duties that bring no joy. Instead of refreshing and ravishing his soul with the love of Christ, his spirituality seems complicated, unfulfilling—like just "one more thing to do" in an over-busy life. And so, if you recognize yourself in this bondage, rest your soul afresh in "the simplicity and purity of devotion to Christ." Look to Him to be the satisfaction of what God requires from you. Rediscover your spiritual practices as the means of experiencing and enjoying Christ and not as a mere checklist of requirements to keep.

But other readers who feel boxed-in spiritually, as far as they know their own hearts, *have* kept their eyes on Christ alone, not only to *make* them right with God, but also to *keep* them right with God. And yet the responsibilities of life have become so overwhelming that even the habits of their spirituality only seem to add to the burden and complexity of their weary existence. Spiritually, they're as dry and rootless as tumbleweed. If this is you, it's my prayer that as you turn these pages, your devotion to Christ will become more simple and pure. And as it does, may you feel the refreshing return of the gentleness and love of Christ in your soul.

Practice True Spirituality

In our quest for a more simple spirituality, it's important to define the term. I'm writing from the belief that spirituality is the pursuit of God and the things of God, through Jesus Christ, by the power of the Holy Spirit, in accordance with God's self-revelation (that is, the Bible).

The words of the apostle Paul in Colossians 2:16–3:2 provide inspired guidance on true spirituality. False teachers in Colossae were saying that spirituality involved not only the pursuit of God through Jesus, but also the worship of angels and other types of mystical experiences. They taught a number of elaborate rituals and ascetic practices which anyone serious about spirituality was required to observe.

Paul admitted that while "these things indeed have an appearance of wisdom in self-imposed religion," in reality they "are of no value against the indulgence of the flesh" (2:23). In other words, these activities may look like marks of true spirituality, but they're worthless for changing one's heart or relationship with God.

But then Paul directs us to the basics of biblical spirituality: "If then you were raised with Christ, seek those things which are above, where Christ is, sitting at the right hand of God. Set your mind on things above, not on things on the earth" (3:1-2).

Unlike the common belief that many people are "spiritual" by nature, notice Paul's teaching that spirituality has a definite starting point: "If then you were raised with Christ." This is biblical language for being united by faith to Jesus Christ in His life, death, and resurrection. Until a person comes to the place where spirituality begins and where he receives the benefits that flow from this union with Christ—namely eternal life and the indwelling presence of the Holy Spirit—that person has no real spirituality, regardless of his effort or desire.

Notice also that genuine spirituality seeks the things of God, or more specifically, "things which are above, where Christ is." Any spirituality that does not seek things like the will and glory of God in everything, intimacy with and conformity to Christ, and love—and does not seek them above all other pursuits—is a false spirituality.

But true spirituality doesn't just propel the heart toward the right activities; it also pulls the mind in the right direction. For in verse 2 Paul continued, "Set your mind on things above, not on things on the earth." True spirituality is characterized by a mind preoccupied with "things above"—and not "things above" merely as we might *imagine* them, but rather as God has *revealed* them in Scripture. This doesn't mean we shouldn't think about earthly things, for Paul himself gives lengthy counsel about such matters just a few verses later, from 3:18 to the end of the book. Rather, the spirituality that flows from Heaven causes "things above" to become a magnet for the mind, so that no matter what we think about, eventually we relate it somehow to "things above." For instance, we often find ourselves asking questions like, "What would the Lord have me do in this situation?" or "What is God's view of this?"

Don't be deceived by a complex spirituality that gives the appearance of wisdom but doesn't start with Christ, "in whom are hidden all the treasures of wisdom and knowledge" (Colossians 2:3). And don't become entangled in any spiritual practices that sound good but incline your mind and heart away from the "things above."

Know Why You Simplify

WHY DO YOU WANT TO SIMPLIFY YOUR SPIRITUAL LIFE? IS IT TO SAVE time? To recover some control over your life? To get organized? Just to be less busy?

All these are worthy pursuits, but they are secondary. The primary reason to pursue simplicity in our spirituality is to maintain "the simplicity and purity of devotion to Christ" (2 Corinthians 11:3, NASB). Every other motivation for simplifying should serve this one.

We simplify, not just to be less busy, even though we may be right to pursue that. Rather, we simplify to remove distractions from our pursuit of Christ. We prune activities from our lives, not only to get organized, but also that our devotion to Christ and service for His kingdom will be more fruitful. We simplify, not merely to save time, but to eliminate hindrances to the time we devote to knowing Christ. All the reasons we simplify should eventually lead us to Jesus Christ.

In her book *Between Walden and the Whirlwind*, author Jean Fleming points to the example of "simplicity and purity of devotion to Christ" in the life and letters of the apostle Paul: "The apostle Paul's obvious center was Christ. His writings never digress from Christ. They ring with the steady, predictable hammer striking the anvil of life: life is *in* Christ, *of* Christ, *through* Christ, *by* Christ, *with* Christ, *for* Christ, *from* Christ. To live is Christ, and to die is more of Christ."[2]

The ultimate reason for all we do should be Christ. Is He the reason you want to simplify your spiritual life?

Remember, It's About Jesus

WHY PRAY WHEN IT APPEARS THAT YOUR PRAYERS GO UNANSWERED? Why keep on reading the Bible when it seems you're getting little from it? Why continue worshiping God privately when you feel no spiritual refreshment? Why persist in keeping a journal when writing your entries bores you? Why engage in fasting, silence and solitude, serving, and other spiritual disciplines when you sense meager benefits from doing so?

It's easy to forget the real purpose of anything that's as habitual as the activities of the spiritual life. And purposeless spiritual practices soon become dry routines that shrivel our souls.

The apostle Paul wrote of his concern that something like this would happen to the Christians at Corinth: "But I am afraid, lest as the serpent deceived Eve by his craftiness, your minds should be led astray from the simplicity and purity of devotion to Christ" (2 Corinthians 11:3, NASB). Notice that the direction of devotion is to be "to Christ." Spirituality is not an end in itself; it's about Jesus.

When we realize just who this God-Man—this Jesus who is called the Christ—is, we understand why the spiritual life is about Him: "And He is the head of the body, the church, who is the beginning, the firstborn from the dead, that in all things He may have the preeminence" (Colossians 1:18). So, "in all things," including our spirituality, Jesus should "have the preeminence."

That's why God inspired Paul to tell us, "Discipline yourself for the purpose of godliness [that is, Christlikeness]" (1 Timothy 4:7, NASB). All our spiritual disciplines should be practiced in pursuit of Christlikeness. We pursue *outward* conformity to Christlikeness as we practice the same disciplines He practiced. More importantly, we pursue intimacy with Jesus and the *inner* transformation to Christlikeness when we look to Him *through* the spiritual disciplines.

So when we go to the Bible, we should look primarily for what Jesus says to us in it, for what it tells us about Jesus, for how we are to respond to Jesus, for what we are to do for Jesus, and so forth. When we pray, we want to pray in Jesus' name (see John 14:13-14); that is, we should come in the righteousness of Jesus (and not our own) and pray what we believe Jesus would pray in our circumstances. Our perennial purpose for practicing any and all of the spiritual disciplines should be a Christ-centered purpose. Authentic *Christ*-ian spirituality is about Jesus Christ.

Take Up Your Cross Daily
and Follow Jesus

During the Protestant Reformation of the 1500s, Martin Luther articulated a timeless distinction between two approaches to knowing God. He labeled one a "theology of glory" and applied it to those who believe they can attain to a glorious knowledge of God by human goodness, religious effort, mystical experiences, or the wisdom of human reason. According to this view, God manifests Himself most often through blessings, victory, success, miracles, power, and other exhilarating experiences of "glory."

By contrast, Luther argued that the biblical way to know God goes through a "theology of the cross." God has "hidden" Himself where human wisdom would not expect to find Him, that is, in the lowliness and suffering of the man Jesus Christ, and especially in His humiliating death on a Roman cross. As Luther put it, "True theology and recognition of God are in the crucified Christ."[3] So rather than finding God by ascending to Him through our efforts, wisdom, or self-initiated experiences, God has descended to us in Jesus, whose glory was in the least expected of places—the cross—and in a way where He can be found by faith alone.

Our natural tendency is to look for Him through the theology of glory. As with the apostle Philip, our way says, "Show us the Father, and it is sufficient for us." But rather than display a vision of the Father in Heaven, Jesus pointed to Himself—a poor, simple man—saying, "He who has seen Me has seen the Father" (John 14:8-9). Our theology of glory says with Jesus' enemies, "Let Him now come down from the cross, and we will believe Him" (Matthew 27:42). And even though He *could* have exploded off the cross in a dazzling display of power and called legions of magnificent angels from Heaven to testify to His deity, Jesus stayed on the cross until His work was finished.

The cross lies at the heart of all God did through Jesus Christ. It is the supreme example of God's power and wisdom displayed in what the world considers weakness and foolishness (see 1 Corinthians 1:18-25). And anyone who wants to know God must find Him in Christ crucified.

But the cross is as central to following Christ daily as it is to knowing Him initially. Notice the word *daily* in the invitation of Jesus: "Then He said to them all, 'If anyone desires to come after Me, let him deny himself, and take up his cross daily, and follow Me'" (Luke 9:23).

As Jesus was willing to go to the cross to do the will of the Father (see Philippians 2:8), so we must be willing to follow Jesus to the cross, daily dying to any desires that conflict with His so that we may daily live for Him. While we may truly speak of the glory inaugurated by the resurrection and ascension of Jesus, identifying with and following Him in this world involves suffering. Indeed, there will be no end to cross-bearing this side of Heaven.

The theology of the cross simplifies the spiritual life by standing as its primary reference point. Everything in Christian spirituality relates to it. Through the cross we *begin* our spirituality, and by the power and example of the cross we *live* it. Ask God to show Himself afresh to you through the Bible's teaching of the cross and where this theology needs fresh application in your life.

Root Your Spirituality in Scripture

A woman told me she'd saved several hundred dollars as a result of acting on a dream. Then she asked, "That had to be God, didn't it?"

It might have been. In any case, God certainly *allowed* the dream. But who can say if He *directly caused* it?

I do not deny that Christians can have such unexpected experiences with God. In fact, I would affirm that the Holy Spirit stirs up thoughts about God and the things of God in the mind of every believer every day.[4] While we are riding in the car, the Spirit may cause us to recall something we heard in a sermon, or to think of the return of Jesus, or to pray for our family or a missionary. Our part is to cultivate these Spirit-initiated thoughts—doing so may lead to wonderful experiences with God. Additionally, there are encounters with the Lord in prayer when He grants a sense of His presence that's almost atmospheric.

These kinds of experiences with God are valid, but by themselves they are unreliable and insufficient. Rather, Scripture-induced meetings with God should have priority in our spirituality. And Scripture alone should be the standard by which all spiritual experiences are evaluated.

Jesus and His apostles didn't urge people to seek dreams or impressions from God; rather, they went about preaching and teaching the Scriptures (see, for example, Mark 1:14-15). Jesus did not say to live by mystical experiences, but rather to "live . . . by every word that proceeds from the mouth of God" (Matthew 4:4). The apostle Peter taught that God has "given to us exceedingly great and precious promises, *that through these* you may be partakers of the divine nature" (2 Peter 1:4, emphasis added).

So, as Scripture itself teaches, the main method of meeting God is *through Scripture*. Through the words of Scripture, the power from Heaven shines a divine and supernatural light into our minds and ignites a passionate love for God in our hearts.

How does this happen? When indwelled by the Holy Spirit, we can hear God speaking through the Bible in ways that nourish us, encourage us, and give us hope like no mortal can. We read of "Christ who is our life" in Colossians 3:4, and while meditating on that, our hearts turn to Christ as flowers to the sun. He refreshes our spirits and evokes our thanksgiving and adoration. His love renews our desire to live for Him and speak of Him. This is the sort of spiritual experience we need regularly, and it comes most reliably when we seek Him through the way He has revealed Himself to us— through Scripture.

All other experiences with God that do not *begin* with Scripture should be *informed* by and *interpreted* by Scripture. So when a breathtaking sunset, the radiance of the stars, the scent of pines, or the laughter of children ushers us into communion with God, let us enjoy Him through it to the full. However, everything we learn, affirm, or enjoy about God in that experience—if it is of God— will agree with what He has already revealed about Himself in Scripture. We may sigh at the beauty of the sunset and exclaim, "God is so good!" The statement is true, not because we feel it, but because the Bible says that God is good. Our experiences do not determine whether the Bible is true; rather, the Bible determines whether our experiences are true.

It simplifies the spiritual life to evaluate all spiritual experiences by a single standard—the Bible.

EMBRACE A TRINITARIAN SPIRITUALITY

I ONCE READ AN ARTICLE THAT QUOTED A TV STAR AS SAYING, "I consider myself a spiritual person." Almost everyone nowadays is "into spirituality." I saw a survey where even a majority of *atheists* consider themselves "spiritual" people. By this I assume they mean they often rely on intuition, consider feelings important in decision making, and try to disassociate themselves from a merely materialistic view of life.

But spirituality is much more than learning to look within one's soul. It goes far beyond just trying to live more by intangible values and principles. True spirituality, in contrast to the popular, self-defined spirituality of today, is above all a God-centered spirituality. Any spirituality without God is just self-worship by another name. It is the ultimate self-centeredness, and in fact, often uses terminology about "centering." But the focus of the centering is upon oneself, not God.

The spirituality of Scripture is a Trinitarian spirituality. Biblical spirituality is centered on the triune God: God the Father who is reached through God the Son who is magnified by God the Holy Spirit.

Jesus taught us that eternal life (the ultimate in spirituality) is knowing the God who is revealed in the Bible. "And this is eternal life," Jesus' disciples heard Him pray, "that they may know You, the only true God, and Jesus Christ whom You have sent" (John 17:3). But He also explicitly maintained that the only way to the Father is through Himself: "I am the way, and the truth, and the life. No one comes to the Father except through Me" (14:6). Further, Jesus said that when He returned to Heaven, the Holy Spirit would come and His role would be to magnify Jesus: "But when the Helper comes, whom I shall send to you from the Father, the Spirit of truth who proceeds from the Father, He will testify of Me" (15:26). In other words, the Spirit will call attention to Jesus and cause those whom He influences to love and obey Jesus.

Any other pseudo-spirituality is merely self-effort, self-love, and empty. It is good to have a zeal for spirituality, but if it's a zeal "not according to knowledge" (Romans 10:2)—that is, the knowledge God gives through His Word—it's a spiritual mirage. It is good to desire a simpler spirituality, but a spirituality that's simpler than that taught in the Bible is simply wrong. So away with any spirituality without God—the one, true God. Away with any spirituality without Jesus Christ and the Holy Spirit. Embrace a Trinitarian spirituality.

Experience Congregational Spirituality

"I want God and spirituality, but not the church."

More people say this today than ever. Spirituality is in; church is out. Why? For some, the painful memories of previous church experiences keep them away. For others, church problems aren't worth the hassle. For many, church just seems irrelevant or unhelpful to their own spirituality. Perhaps most would simply say, "I'm too busy for church."

The Bible specifically addresses a churchless view of spirituality. To begin with, a person who wants God, but not the church, needs to come to grips with 1 John 3:14: "We know that we have passed from death to life, because we love the brethren." A sacrificial love for Christian brothers and sisters is one of the first, best, and most reliable evidences of having passed from spiritual death into eternal life through Christ. Anyone who claims to possess this love for God's people, but avoids their regular gatherings, needs to reexamine his relationship with the Father of this family.

Second, anyone who calls Jesus "Lord" must submit to the authority of His Word when it warns against "forsaking the assembling of ourselves together, as is the manner of some" (Hebrews 10:25). The New Testament knows nothing of the individualized spirituality of today and nothing of a Christianity that exists apart from the local church.

Remember too that the church is Jesus' idea, not man's. More than that, the church is His body. The apostle Paul reminds us, "Christ is head of the church; and He is Savior of the body," and "we are members of His body" (Ephesians 5:23,30). Even though it may sometimes appear otherwise, the body of Christ has not been severed from its Head; Jesus is still the Head of the church. Why wouldn't anyone want to actively participate in the only organization on earth where Jesus Christ is the Head? When one of His earliest promises was, "I will build My church" (Matthew 16:18), why wouldn't anyone want a part in what Jesus Himself is building?

Look at Jesus' own example. He wasn't a spiritual loner. Twelve disciples always traveled with Him, often teaching and ministering as well. Furthermore, Luke 4:16 reminds us that, "as His custom was, He went into the synagogue on the Sabbath day." Why did Jesus make it His custom to go to the synagogue every Sabbath? Because He would hear the Word of God, worship God, and fellowship with His people there.

That's how participation in congregational spirituality builds our individual spirituality. When we're fed by the preaching and teaching of Scripture, receive the Lord's Supper, sing praises and pray with Christ's people, and talk about the things of God together, the Spirit strengthens us in ways that do not occur when we're alone.

So attend, join, worship in, learn in, give to, fellowship with, and spiritually thrive in a local body of Christ that's faithful to God's Word. Find teachers and models there who can help with simplifying your spiritual life. Failing that, consider starting some type of small group in the church to discuss or study a book on the subject.

Christian spirituality is not an isolationist, self-absorbed spirituality. True spirituality is relational—not only toward God, but also with the people of God. Proverbs 18:1 teaches, "A man who isolates himself seeks his own desire; he rages against all wise judgment." Don't isolate yourself from the people of God. Take God, spirituality, *and* the church. That's God's plan. His ways are simpler and healthier for our souls than any we contrive on our own.

Don't Mistake Simplicity for Heaven

You'd expect a book on spirituality to devote at least a little space to the subject of Heaven. And it's especially appropriate when the book is about the simplifying of spirituality. That's because some of the literature of the simplicity movement would lead us to believe that a simple lifestyle is Heaven itself. But simplicity is not Heaven; only *Heaven* is Heaven.

Much of the search for simplicity is actually a pursuit for something found only in Heaven. Within our hearts beats a desire for a much better world. God made our hearts, including the longings within them. And He designed our deepest and most enduring longings to point us in the direction of their unimaginably glorious fulfillment with Himself in Heaven.

However, we're prone to believe that if we can accumulate the right combination of people, things, and activities, then our heart's longings will be satisfied. So like Solomon (see especially Ecclesiastes 1:12–2:17), we turn from one pursuit to another, thinking that the next one will bring the happiness and fulfillment we crave. But no matter who or what we get, no matter what we experience, we soon realize that he, she, or it doesn't bring the perfect satisfaction we're after. Also like Solomon, we keep discovering that "under the sun . . . all is vanity and grasping for the wind" (1:14; 2:17).

Then in the midst of our pursuits for happiness we become convinced that the missing ingredient is simplicity. And it's true that God through Scripture directs us toward a kind of simplicity. For instance, Jesus instructs us to "seek first the kingdom of God and His righteousness, and all these things [like food, drink, and clothing] shall be added to you" (Matthew 6:33). And if we'll live this way, we'll enjoy the most rewarding life possible in this world.

But here's where some misunderstand the potential of simplicity. Not even the most thorough and biblical simplicity can return us to the Garden of Eden, much less bring Heaven on earth. For we're still sinful people leading these simplified lives, lives that remain intertwined with and influenced by other sinful people. Besides that, the world, the flesh, and the Devil sinfully complicate all our efforts at simplifying. This evil trio ensures that even the best and most simple lives still feel many pressures, frustrations, problems, and disappointments.

Should we then forsake our quest for simplicity? No, we don't stop trying just because we can't get all we want from simplifying. To do so would be like saying we should stop loving because we'll never experience perfect love in this world. We must remember, though, that a simpler life and spirituality is not paradise—Heaven is.

Let's simplify, for it's a more God-glorifying, more kingdom-seeking, more satisfying way to live. Let's simplify where we can and as much as we can, but always look "unto Jesus . . . who for the joy that was set before Him endured the cross, despising the shame, and has sat down at the right hand of the throne of God" (Hebrews 12:2).

As with Jesus, our simplicity will also mean enduring crosses. The blessings of simplicity, sweet as they are, come mixed with thorns and troubles. Let's not be surprised or disillusioned by them. The real joy—the unmixed, indescribable, eternal joy—is yet to come. Pursue simplicity, but press on to the real Heaven.

Simplify Your Spiritual Life
Without Misconceptions

When you start simplifying your spiritual life, it's easy to fall prey to some misconceptions. Watch out for these.

Misconception #1—Simplifying the spiritual life eliminates the need for spiritual discipline. The Bible teaches that if your purpose is Christlikeness (and it is, if you are a Christian), then discipline is the God-given means to it. "Discipline yourself," said the apostle Paul, "for the purpose of godliness" (1 Timothy 4:7, NASB). We don't simplify our spiritual lives in order to avoid the spiritual disciplines, but to practice them more fruitfully.[5]

Misconception #2—Simplifying the spiritual life will simplify the rest of life. The spiritual life is the eternal and most important part of life, but it is not the only part. So while there may be progress in simplifying our spirituality, other segments of life may remain intensely complicated. Our work, finances, or family schedule, for example, may be way too complex, even while our spirituality is growing less so. But the spiritual life is the best place to start simplifying all of life. Any transformation there has the power to affect everything else we do.

Misconception #3—Simplifying the spiritual life is a one-time event. Though we simplify and enjoy smooth sailing in our spirituality, we inevitably attract the old and new complexities of life like barnacles. The fresh, clean space that simplifying creates in our spiritual life will not stay that way without vigilance. Simplifying—in any part of life—tends to be an ongoing process.

Misconception #4—Simplifying the spiritual life is to minimize the spiritual life. This is the view that the way to simplify the spiritual life is just to cut back on the time devoted to spirituality. "So," such a person reasons, "I can simplify my spiritual life by reading the Bible less, or praying less. And if I really want to simplify I won't read Scripture or pray at all." I suppose it's possible that some need to spend less time devoted to things of the soul and of the next world, and devote more time to temporal matters, but I've never met them. The question to address is not how to spend less time devoted exclusively to spiritual pursuits, but how to spend that time better.

By avoiding these misconceptions we can also avoid some of the disillusionment that sometimes occurs when simplifying the spiritual life.

Beware of Simplifying

ALTHOUGH THE TITLE OF THIS BOOK IS *SIMPLIFY YOUR SPIRITUAL Life,* I urge you to beware of simplifying.

If I had to pick a theme verse for this book, I'd choose 2 Corinthians 11:3, where the apostle Paul said, "But I am afraid, lest as the serpent deceived Eve by his craftiness, your minds should be led astray from the simplicity and purity of devotion to Christ" (NASB). What Paul feared for his readers in Corinth still happens today. One of the ways it could happen to some who read this book might surprise you. To say it the way Paul put it, "I am afraid that your minds will be led astray *by simplicity* from the simplicity and purity of devotion to Christ."

There's a kind of cult of simplicity today, and no wonder. While life has always been hard, never has it been more hectic and complicated than now. As Richard A. Swenson reminds us in *Margin* and *The Overload Syndrome,* the result of "progress" in technology and the economy is the production of more and more of everything faster and faster. Inevitably, though, the rapid accumulation of it all—including even many of the good things in life, such as the ability to travel or communicate ever quicker—begins to overwhelm us. As our physical, emotional, relational, financial, and spiritual reserves become depleted, we desperately search for relief. Simplifying our lives sounds like the answer. Consequently, the "simplicity movement" gains momentum every day. Books, magazines, websites, newsletters, retreats, conferences, courses, study groups, and communities devoted to simplicity multiply daily.

Beware, however, when simplifying begins to overgrow its purpose. Instead of serving the spiritual life, simplifying can gradually take over as master. For some, simplifying no longer assists their spiritual life; it *is* their spiritual life. Models of a simple lifestyle like Henry David Thoreau become their messiahs, and books like *Walden* their Bible.

Just like any other passion or pursuit, simplifying can become an idol. It takes thought and energy to simplify, and it's easy for it to start siphoning some of our devotion to Christ. With all its benefits, simplifying has the deceptive potential to make us even more materialistic, earthbound, and self-centered. That's because those most serious about simplifying never stop evaluating what things they need and what things they can live without, or thinking about ways to save money and get things cheaper.

I've read—and profited from—a bit of the literature of the simplicity movement. There's much good there. Don't forget, however, what simplifying cannot do. Simplifying your life cannot save your soul. Some people's zealous efforts to simplify are nothing more than a well-intentioned violation of Jesus' words in Matthew 16:25: "For whoever desires to save his life will lose it." To paraphrase the next verse, "For what profit is it to a man if he [simplifies] the whole world, and loses his own soul?"

Simplify wherever needed; but beware of being led astray *by simplicity* from the simplicity and purity of devotion to Christ.

Beware of Progress

One of the warnings in Richard A. Swenson's *Margin* and *The Overload Syndrome* is about the unexpected consequences of "progress." Although it promises to make life simpler, progress invariably leads to more complexity and frustration. Listen to Swenson:

> Margin has been stolen away, and progress is the thief.[6]

> Progress always gives us *more and more of everything faster and faster.* . . . There are only so many details that can be comfortably managed in anybody's life. Once this number has been exceeded, one of two things happens: disorganization or frustration. Yet progress gives us more and more details every year—often at exponential rates. We have to deal with more "things per person" than ever before in the history of humankind. . . . Every year we have more products, more information, more technology, more activities, more choices, more change, more traffic, more commitments, more work. In short, more of everything. Faster. This ubiquitous overloading is a natural function of progress. It is automatic. *Progress automatically leads to increasing overload, marginlessness, speed, change, stress, and complexity.*[7]

> If we want margin back, we will first have to do something about progress.[8]

> If we sit meekly and do nothing about it, next year at this time, we will be even more overloaded than we are right now. . . .

Progress is not going to slow down. We can count on more and more from here on out.[9]

Contentment and simplicity . . . will help. Abiding by scriptural teaching concerning money, possessions, education, and priorities will help immensely.[10]

Preventing the tendency of progress to erode our most important relationships will also help. Swenson says, "Progress's biggest failure has been its inability to nurture and protect right relationships,"[11] including our relationships with family, friends, church, and most importantly, God.

Let's ensure that the nonstop spiral of the world's economic and technological progress doesn't cause us to forget that God is more interested in the progress of our relationships with Him and with people. As the nineteenth-century Christian statesman William Wilberforce put it, "Above all, measure your progress by your experience of the love of God and its exercise before men."[12]

Do All to the Glory of God

THE UNIFYING PRINCIPLE FOR ALL OF LIFE, INCLUDING OUR SPIRITU-
ality, is found in 1 Corinthians 10:31: "Therefore, whether you eat
or drink, or whatever you do, do all to the glory of God." This is the
sun around which every spiritual practice, every decision, every
prayer, and everything else—including our efforts at simplifying—
should revolve.

Concern for the glory of God in all things was the heartbeat of
God's Son, Jesus. When only one of ten lepers (and he a Samaritan)
whom Jesus had cleansed returned to thank Him, Jesus said, "Were
there not ten cleansed? But where are the nine? Were there not any
found who returned to *give glory to God* except this foreigner?" (Luke
17:17-18, emphasis added here and following). Jesus wasn't indig-
nant because He received so little thanks for healing these men. He
wasn't thinking of Himself; rather, He was jealous over the lack of
glory God received for this wonderful miracle.

According to John 12:27-28, Jesus has realized that the time for
His arrest and crucifixion is at hand. Knowing He will soon die
under the wrath of God, listen to His primary concern: "Now My
soul is troubled, and what shall I say? 'Father, save Me from this
hour'? But for this purpose I came to this hour. *Father, glorify Your
name.*" A short time later, just hours before He was taken into cus-
tody, Jesus taught us to ask in His name when we pray. Notice the
reason why He promises such prayers will be answered: "And whatever you ask in My name, that I will do, *that the Father may be glorified in the Son*" (John 14:13). The passion that propelled the entire
life and ministry of Jesus Christ was His zeal for the glory of God.

From matters as crucial as the death of Jesus, to those as mundane as eating and drinking, the Bible presents the glory of God as

the ultimate priority and the definitive criterion by which we should evaluate everything. So when faced with choices about how to simplify your spiritual life, ask first, "Which choice(s) will bring the most glory to God?" Simplify in such a way "that in all things *God may be glorified through Jesus Christ*, to whom belong the glory and the dominion forever and ever" (1 Peter 4:11).

SIMPLIFYING
AND
THE
TRUTH

Rely on the Authority
and Guidance of Scripture

"I like to think of Heaven this way."

"I've always imagined Heaven to be a place where . . . "

"To me, Heaven is like . . . "

Have you noticed how people want to take biblical terms, empty them of biblical content, and fill them with their own meaning? Take Heaven, for instance. Everyone wants to go to the biblical place called Heaven, but many reject the qualifications for Heaven declared in the Bible and show no interest in the Bible's description of Heaven's activities.

People also tend to repackage the truth about the nature of God and spirituality. They imagine God as they want Him to be ("Well, *my* God isn't like that!"), despite what God has revealed about Himself in the Bible. And people want to relate to God through their own self-determined kind of spirituality. But God has established His Word—the Bible—as the final authority and infallible guide for true and eternal spirituality.

One reason we should accept the authority and guidance of the Bible is because it is God's self-revelation to us. God is "the King eternal, immortal, invisible" (1 Timothy 1:17). And unless our invisible Creator revealed Himself to us, we would know nothing about Him. How could we? Anything we might say about Him would be pure speculation. Someone could claim that God has a body of green flesh, three heads, and stands one hundred feet tall. How would he prove that claim, or anyone else prove otherwise? The only completely trustworthy source of information about the nature of God, knowing God, and how to relate to God in our spirituality is the self-revelation of God we call the Bible.

This is why God tells us throughout the Bible to search it for guidance in all things, especially our spirituality. But shouldn't we look to the real-life spiritual experiences of people as equal in authority to the Bible? As helpful as those might be to us, the prophet Isaiah answers, "To the law and to the testimony! If they do not speak according to this word, it is because there is no light in them" (Isaiah 8:20).

As a guide for our spirituality, "The law of the Lord is perfect . . . sure . . . right . . . pure . . . clean . . . true and righteous altogether" (Psalm 19:7-9). The Bible's counsel for our spiritual life is not just a collection of ancient wisdom; rather as Jesus put it, "The words that I speak to you are spirit, and they are life" (John 6:63). So Scripture guides our spiritual life by more than mere "principles," but by a real, supernatural power, "for the word of God is living and powerful . . . and is a discerner of the thoughts and intents of the heart" (Hebrew 4:12). All this is so because "all Scripture is given by inspiration of God" (2 Timothy 3:16).

Who but God can tell us about God and guide us in our experience with God? He does so in the Bible. Rely on it.

ASK OFTEN, "WHAT DOES THE BIBLE SAY?"

SOME OF THE MOST IMPORTANT CHANGES IN MY LIFE OCCURRED when I thought to ask, "What does the Bible say about this?" The way I spend the Lord's Day, for example, and my thinking about what activities please God in worship were dramatically changed when I purposed to study what God's Word said about those matters.

Far more often than we do, Christians should ask such questions. In our relationships, finances, use of time, priorities, parenting, simplifying, and everything else, we should more quickly ask, "What does the Bible say about this?"

The wisdom of frequently asking this question is obvious if we believe truths like these:

- "The testimony of the Lord is sure, making wise the simple" (Psalm 19:7).
- "Your word is a lamp to my feet and a light to my path" (Psalm 119:105).
- "Man shall not live by bread alone, but by every word that proceeds from the mouth of God" (Matthew 4:4).
- "All Scripture is given by inspiration of God, and is profitable for doctrine, for reproof, for correction, for instruction in righteousness, that the man of God may be complete, thoroughly equipped for every good work" (2 Timothy 3:16-17).

Nothing will simplify our lives more than finding the will of God on a matter and doing it. And the best way to discover the will of God is to search the Word of God.

What's the most significant issue in your life right now? What major decision is before you? Be sure to ask, "What does the Bible say about this?" Then, as you turn to the Bible, pray the prayer of Psalm 119:18: "Open my eyes, that I may see wondrous things from Your law."

Go to the Scriptures for Patience, Comfort, and Hope

On most mornings I turn to the Scriptures as much out of a good, lifelong habit as anything else. On some mornings I approach God's Word with a more keen sense of purpose. And sometimes I come with a real desire to meet God. But on many occasions—often outside my daily routine of Bible intake—I turn to the Word of God out of an acute awareness of *need*. The world's increasing complexity may have tensed my anxiety and frustration levels close to the snapping point. Or suffering, finances, or circumstances may have drained all my courage, endurance, or heart. At such times we should go to the Bible and ask the Lord to give us patience, comfort, and hope through His Word.

We can do so with confidence, because the Bible expressly says, "For whatever things were written before were written for our learning, that we through the patience and comfort of the Scriptures might have hope" (Romans 15:4).

When the apostle Paul spoke of things "written before," he was referring to what we now call the Old Testament. Today we can affirm that "whatever things were written before" applies to the New Testament as well. The whole Bible was written "for our learning," that is, to instruct us—chiefly about God and His glory, and His work through Jesus Christ. And through these Scriptures, God gives real "patience and comfort [and] hope."

Every now and then my heart is so broken, or my grief so deep, or my burden so heavy that I drop down in my desk chair, open the Bible, put my head in my hands and cry out, "O Father, please comfort me through Your Word." Or, "Lord, I'm so discouraged. I don't know if I can go on. Give me hope!"

How does He answer? Sometimes it's through promises, "I will never leave you nor forsake you" (Hebrews 13:5). Or He answers through the assurances of doctrinal passages like Romans 8:18: "For I consider that the sufferings of this present time are not worthy to be compared with the glory which shall be revealed in us." Or He may reply through the comfort of psalms penned by writers with the same passions as those coursing through my soul: "Why are you cast down, O my soul? And why are you disquieted within me? Hope in God, for I shall yet praise Him for the help of His countenance" (Psalm 42:5).

Overall, I think God means for us to draw patience, comfort, and hope from the Scriptures by seeing there how He has always accomplished His purposes throughout the world and at all times, and then believing that He will accomplish them in our lives. I can read the Old Testament, and then see how God fulfilled it in Jesus Christ and the church. I can read in the New Testament of both the power of Christ and His tender mercies toward His own. Then I encounter the repeated promises that Jesus will return for His people and take us to an eternal home of joy more glorious than all the sunsets in the history of the world combined. Through these holy, historic, and living words, God grants patience with His timing and providence in my life. Through these God-breathed lines, I experience the comfort of His presence and precious promises. And in the pages of Scripture, He gives me the hope of a better world that is one day closer.

In His mercy, the Lord encourages us through people, circumstances, and countless other ways. But there's no simpler, purer, or more direct means of receiving His patience, comfort, or hope than by going to His Word and asking for it.

Use a Bible Reading Plan

IMAGINE PICKING UP A HISTORY OF THE UNITED STATES AND STARTING with the chapter on the Great Depression. Finishing that, then suppose you turn to read of the War of 1812, and then of putting Neil Armstrong on the moon. Or picture yourself taking the biography of George Washington off the shelf and reading first of his marriage to Martha, then a chapter on his final years, and then the one on the general's initial military campaign.

Not a good way to understand either history or someone's life, is it?

But that's how some people read the Bible. A chapter of Genesis today, one from Romans tomorrow, a couple of psalms the next day—such a haphazard approach is not the way to understand the message of Scripture.

To read the Bible purposefully requires a plan. The plan can be as simple as starting in Genesis and reading a certain number of chapters each day straight through to Revelation, or as involved as reading in multiple books at a sitting.

A good plan is easy to find. Many study Bibles (the kind with lots of explanatory notes at the bottoms of pages and other resources throughout) have Bible reading plans included at the back. Devotional magazines and church Bible study literature often print daily readings on each page that will direct you through the entire Bible in a year. With very little effort you will find the plan developed by a godly Scottish minister in the 1800s, Robert Murray McCheyne, which is one of the most widely used in the world. You can even buy a Bible specially printed in a format for daily reading instead of in the traditional Genesis-to-Revelation arrangement.

My favorite plan takes the reader through five parts of Scripture per session. On the first of January I read in Genesis (the Law), then an equal amount in Joshua (History), Job (Poetry), Isaiah (the Prophets), and Matthew (the New Testament). I read consecutively through each section, and since each is approximately the same length, I finish them all about the same time. A variation on the plan is to read equal amounts daily in three sections, beginning in Genesis, Job, and Matthew.

The advantage of any plan that guides the reader through more than one book of the Bible per sitting is variety. On the days when part of your reading is in the more difficult passages, it's easier to maintain the momentum when you know you'll also be reading from other parts of the Bible as well.

Jesus said, "Man shall not live by bread alone, but by every word that proceeds from the mouth of God" (Matthew 4:4). If we are to *live* by "every word that proceeds from the mouth of God," then surely He intends for us to at least *read* every word. And the best way to do that is with the help of a Bible reading plan.

Even if, however, you aren't currently attempting to read through the entire Bible, but are reading books at random, there's no better—or simpler—way than chapter by chapter, book by book, in a purposeful and orderly method.

Establish Bible Reading Routines

When I was in my twenties, I first heard someone call attention to the fact that there are thirty-one chapters in the book of Proverbs, one for each day of the month. He made it a daily habit—in addition to his other Bible reading—to read the chapter that corresponds to the day of the month. Accepting his recommendation into my own daily Bible reading routines was one of the best pieces of advice I've ever taken. The Lord has guided me by means of the practical wisdom of Proverbs on countless occasions.

Ten years later, I realized I could approach the longest chapter in the Bible, Psalm 119, in a similar way, reading one of the twenty-two, eight-verse sections on each of the first twenty-two days of the month. In this way I am regularly reminded (as I was today) of the value of the Word of God and how it should be "hidden in my heart" (verse 11).

About the same time, I added the book of Ecclesiastes to my Bible reading routines. These twelve chapters are very similar to Proverbs, and I began receiving the same kinds of blessings in them that I enjoyed in reading through the longer book. So, during the last week of each month, I read one or two chapters each day, finishing the book on the last day of the month.

Then after another ten years I heard someone describe the book of James as the "Proverbs of the New Testament" because of its similarities with the Old Testament wisdom literature. Because my portion of Psalm 119 consisted of only eight verses a day, after that brief passage I began turning to James and reading one paragraph there. On many mornings these daily doses of "the wisdom that is from above" (James 3:17), taken in bite-size chunks, have been exactly the divine nourishment my soul needed.

Before this, when I was still a full-time pastor, I developed the habit of reading a chapter each day from one of the three Pastoral Epistles (that is, the letters written especially for ministers). Referring to these instructions given by God through him, the apostle Paul wrote, "Meditate on these things; give yourself entirely to them" (1 Timothy 4:15). One of the simplest ways I've found of obeying this Scripture is to cycle repeatedly through the thirteen chapters of these three letters of 1–2 Timothy and Titus. There's no reason why every minister couldn't profit from the ongoing consideration of these God-inspired words about how he "ought to conduct [himself] in the house of God, which is the church" (1 Timothy 3:15).

Regardless of whether you are ready at present to add any of these routines to your regular Bible reading schedule, they demonstrate an easy way to work much-needed books or chapters of Scripture into your soul. And if you ever find your sensitivity to one of them dulled by sheer repetition, devote that segment of your daily reading to the enjoyment of other parts of the Bible until you can return to your routine with eager eyes.

In one sense, of course, we all need all of God's Word all the time. If, however, you sense that one or more particular sections of Scripture would be especially beneficial for you, consider making them part of your ongoing daily Bible reading routines.

Connect Spirit with Truth

When it comes to spirituality, you do what you do because you believe what you believe. Regardless of the importance you consciously place upon it, theology drives and determines your spirituality. For example, you pray the way you do because of your theology. And there are certain ways you do *not* pray, more because of theology than tradition.

Recognize, therefore, the connection between good theology and good spirituality. Don't turn to people as models and teachers of spirituality if you could not also turn to them as mentors of theology and doctrine. For *their* spirituality is also connected to their theology.

It's very easy to be impressed by someone's piety and think, "Surely anyone who is so pious, so devoted, and so committed to prayer, couldn't be very wrong in his theology." But I have seen more than one person come to reject biblical theology—even regarding the doctrine of salvation—after he became impressed with the spirituality of a particular writer or speaker who eventually led him astray. As Jesus said, "Take heed what you hear" (Mark 4:24).

So,

- If anyone makes experience authoritative over the revelation of God in Scripture—turn away from him.
- If anyone adds another book or experience to the Bible, making it equal in authority to God's Word—refuse to believe him.
- If anyone teaches that God can be experienced directly, that is, without the mediation of Jesus Christ and the Bible—don't listen to him.

- If anyone says that there are many paths to God and that Jesus isn't the only way to Heaven—avoid him.

Each of us needs *both* sound theology *and* passionate spirituality, because theology is the fuel for spirituality's fire. Theology provides the discernment to protect us from unbiblical or unhealthy spiritual practices (such as regularly seeking to experience God without the guidance or influence of Scripture). Theology can protect us from fads in spirituality.

How do you pursue theology? Read and meditate on Scripture. Listen to biblical preaching and avail yourself of the opportunities for Christian education at your church. Read Christian books that teach, not just those that entertain. These include not only books about doctrine, but also biographies of those who were, like Apollos, "mighty in the Scriptures" (Acts 18:24).

Theology is God's truth. Don't try to grow your soul or simplify your spiritual life without it.

Spontaneously Sing Psalms

I WAS PRAYING THROUGH PSALM 68 IN THE NEW AMERICAN Standard Bible recently. When I came to the words, "Sing to God, sing praises to His name" (verse 4), guess what I did? Yes, I did exactly what the text said. The words of the Bible are not merely to be observed, but also to be obeyed.

But I did more than just "sing to God." I praised Him by singing words quoted from or suggested by this psalm. I sang them to a simple, spontaneous tune that I improvised moment by moment.

> I sing to You, Lord
> I sing praises to Your name (from verse 4)
> Desert Rider (from verse 4)
> Burden Bearer (from verse 19)
> You are a God who is a God of deliverances (from verse 20)

I make no pretense to being a composer, and you'll never hear my melody in church, but this brief song was, I believe, beautiful in God's ears. After all, it came from words He Himself sent to earth with the intention that we would send them back to Heaven. In other words, God has ultimately intended the words of this psalm for *His* ears.

Sometimes you may want to sing His words back to Him in a manner as simple as I did with Psalm 68. If you play an instrument, you might enjoy incorporating it into your improvisational praises to the Lord. Or you may want to sing a psalm just as you find it, singing word for word in a way similar to chanting. Another option is to use a Psalter (a songbook based on the Psalms) or search the

Scripture index at the back of your hymnal for those songs based on Psalms.

Here are ten reasons why it's good to sing from the Psalms when you are alone before the Lord:

1. It's good because the Bible says it's "good to sing praises to our God" (Psalm 147:1).
2. It's good because it helps you to "sing to Him a new song," which the Bible commands in verses such as Psalm 33:3 (see also Psalm 96:1; 98:1; 149:1).
3. It's good because the Bible says to sing "psalms and hymns and spiritual songs" (Ephesians 5:19; Colossians 3:16).
4. It's good because it nourishes your soul as only the words God inspired for us to sing can do.
5. It's good because it expresses to the Lord what's in your heart in a divinely appointed way.
6. It's good because singing God's Word reinforces His truth in your heart and mind.
7. It's good because, along with your mind, it involves your body and soul, making for a more whole-person worship of God.
8. It's good because you learn to express yourself biblically.
9. It's good because it's enlivening to your soul to sing words that are "living and powerful" (Hebrews 4:12).
10. It's good because you unite with what the people of God throughout the world have sung for thousands of years.

It really is "good to sing praises to our God." Enjoy the goodness.

Read *and* Meditate

Have you ever read a few chapters in your Bible, closed it, and then realized, "I don't remember a thing I've read"? When this happens, don't blame your age, IQ, or education, for they're not the cause. Nearly all Bible readers frequently experience this forgetfulness. In most cases, however, the problem has more to do with the *method* of engaging God's Word than anything else. For if you merely read the Bible, don't be surprised if you forget most—if not all—of what you've read.

What's the simple solution? (And I do believe that benefiting from the intake of God's Word *must* be fundamentally simple because the Lord expects it of all His people, regardless of age, IQ, or education.) The solution is not only to read the Scriptures, but to *meditate* on them. Reading, of course, is the starting place. *Reading* is the *exposure* to Scripture, but *meditation* is the *absorption* of Scripture. And it's the absorption of Scripture that leads to the transformation of our lives.

The Bible itself explicitly warns that if we do not look intently at (that is, meditate on) God's perfect Word, we'll forget it: "But one who looks intently at the perfect law, the law of liberty, and abides by it, not having become a forgetful hearer but an effectual doer, this man will be blessed in what he does" (James 1:25, NASB). Just as *hearing* the Word of God without meditating on it causes a person to be a "forgetful hearer," so anyone who *reads* the Bible without meditating on it becomes a forgetful reader. And if you can't remember what you read, you probably won't experience or be changed by what you read.

On most days though, you probably feel as though you're not able to give nearly enough time to the Word of God, much less introduce something else to the process. So, assuming that you're already devoting time on a regular basis to reading the Bible (and if you're not, *that's* the place to start), let me suggest a way whereby you can begin to meditate on Scripture without necessarily increasing the overall time involved.

If, for example, you normally spend ten minutes in Bible reading, from now on don't spend your entire time reading. Starting tomorrow, read for five minutes and meditate for five minutes. It's far better to *read less* but *remember more* than to read for the entire ten minutes and remember nothing. It's far better to close your Bible knowing that you have something from God's Word with you so that you can "meditate in it day and night" (Joshua 1:8) than to realize that you've already forgotten everything you've read.

I've written at length in other places about how to meditate on Scripture.[1] I have space here only to emphasize the importance of meditation. It's not so much what we read in the Bible that changes us, but what we remember. Doubtless there are many believers who should increase their daily intake of Scripture, but many others are devoting all the time they can. If you cannot possibly add meditation to the time you already spend reading, then read less in order to meditate more. The goal is not just to "get through" a certain amount of pages, but to meet God and hear from Him.

Meditate on Scripture and Life

The Bible directs us to four objects of meditation. The one mentioned most often is meditation on *God's Word*. For instance, the "blessed" man of Psalm 1:2 meditates "in His [that is, God's] law." The writer of Psalm 119 repeatedly refers to meditating on God's written revelation (see verses 15, 23, 48, 78, 97, 99, and 148).

A second object of meditation is *God's creation*. This is what King David means in Psalm 143:5 when he says, "I meditate on all Your works."

Third, the Bible also speaks of meditation on *God's providence*. We see this in texts such as Psalm 77:12, which says, "I will also meditate on all Your work, and talk of Your deeds."

Fourth, Scripture points to the practice of meditation on *God's character*. Again, it is King David who illustrates this by testifying, "I meditate on *You* in the night watches" (Psalm 63:6, emphasis added).

These four, however, could be condensed to only two categories: meditation on the *content* of Scripture and meditation on the *perspective* of Scripture. In other words, meditation can focus either on the words of the Bible itself or on another subject from a biblical point of view. I refer to one as "meditation on Scripture" and to the other as "meditation on life from a scriptural perspective."

To meditate on Scripture, I might choose a particular verse from my daily Bible reading and use any of a number of meditation methods. Suppose I read 2 Corinthians 5 tomorrow morning. I could select verse 21 and use "the Joseph Hall questions" mentioned on page 72 to reflect on, "For He made Him who knew no sin to be sin for us, that we might become the righteousness of God in Him." Then at some point I would look for an appropriate way to apply or respond to this part of God's truth.

To meditate on life from a scriptural perspective, I could think about literally any subject that interests me, such as a breathtaking mountain view or a forest of maples in fall foliage. Or I could muse about something that burdens me ("Why is this happening to me?"), or troubles me ("What should I do?"), or anything else that attracts my attention. Eventually, however, I consider what the Bible says about the matter. For instance, I might ask "the Philippians 4:8 questions" about the matter, or simply ponder, "What does the Bible say about this?" I might finally conclude something like, "I don't yet see any reason why God has allowed this to happen, but I 'know that all things work together for good to those who love God, to those who are the called according to His purpose'" (Romans 8:28).

So one form of biblical meditation starts with Scripture and then applies it to life. The other starts with life—something in your heart, family, garden, church, job, country, or world—and then takes it to the light of Scripture.

According to the Bible, all transformation into Christlikeness— including transformation to a simpler spiritual life—involves "the renewing of [the] mind" (Romans 12:2). One of the best pathways to "the renewing of the mind" and thus to simplifying your spiritual life is biblical meditation; that is, meditation on God's truth and meditation on life from the perspective of God's truth.

Meditate for Light and Heat

Central to a simpler spiritual life is doing the will of God. While all Christians know they should do the will of God, there are two common reasons we often do *not* do the will of God. Sometimes it's because we don't *know* God's will, and sometimes it's because we don't *feel* like doing it. Often the simple answer to both problems is meditation on God's Word.

The Bible clearly links meditation to obeying the will of God. We see this in passages such as Joshua 1:8 where the Lord said to Joshua, "This Book of the Law shall not depart from your mouth, but you shall meditate in it day and night, *that* [that is, in order that] you may observe to *do* according to all that is written in it. For then you will make your way prosperous, and then you will have good success" (emphasis added). Likewise, God tells us in James 1:25, "But one who looks *intently* at the perfect law, the law of liberty, *and abides by it,* not having become a forgetful hearer but an effectual doer, this man will be blessed in what he does" (NASB, emphasis added).

Notice the sequence. In both verses, meditation *on* Scripture precedes obedience *to* Scripture. An occasion in the life of King David illustrates how this works. He wanted to speak angrily to someone, but didn't. The more he thought about the situation, the more his heart blazed with anger. He describes it this way in Psalm 39:3: "While I was musing, the fire burned."

There's another and more holy kind of inner fire that can burn within us. "'Is not My word like a fire?' says the Lord" (Jeremiah 23:29). As King David experienced a growing fire within him as he meditated upon it, so our meditation on the fire of God's Word causes it to burn with more intensity in our experience. Meditation works like a bellows on the fire of Scripture. As it does, both spiritual light and spiritual heat increasingly emanate from the fiery Word.

As we receive more spiritual light, we better understand the meaning of a text and how to apply it. "That's what it means! Now I get it," we find ourselves saying more often.

Much of the time, however, our problem in obeying the Bible is not that we don't know what to do; rather, we just don't feel like doing it. We know, for example, that we should turn off the TV or the computer, or that we should speak to someone about Christ, but we just don't feel like it. This need for spiritual zeal is one of the main reasons we need to meditate on the Bible. The fire of Scripture rarely warms our hearts to action when we merely read it. But meditation upon our reading heats the passion of our obedience. The temperature of our spiritual zeal for doing the will of God rises as the bellows of meditation blows upon the flaming Word of God.

If the hindrances to a simpler spiritual life for you include a struggle to know the will of God and do it, meditate on Scripture for light and heat.

Meditate and Apply

All exposure to the Word of God should be followed by absorption of the Word of God. We profit most from our hearing, reading, studying, or memorizing of Scripture when we meditate on some aspect of the text we've encountered. Otherwise, most of the water of the Word will run off the mind and heart like a hard rain on hard ground.

Moreover, the goal of both our exposure to and absorption of Scripture should be our application of Scripture. God commanded Joshua to meditate "day and night" on the law of God left to him by Moses, so that Joshua would *"do* according to all that is written in it" (Joshua 1:8, emphasis added).

Similarly, in the New Testament we find: "But one who looks intently at the perfect law, the law of liberty, and abides by it, not having become a forgetful hearer but an effectual doer, this man will be blessed in what he does" (James 1:25, NASB). The blessing of God in this passage is not promised to those who merely look at—that is, read—God's Word, but to the "one who looks *intently,*" who meditates on what he reads. The blessing does not come, however, until this meditation matures into application. Or as James put it, when "the one who looks intently at the perfect law . . . abides by it, not having become a forgetful hearer but an effectual doer." For it is only in the doing (applying) of Scripture that we become more like Christ and bring the most glory to God.

Of course, the Lord doesn't call us to be just doers of the Word of God in general. He wants us to apply every individual part of it. So one simple way of combining your responsibility both to meditate on and apply the Bible is this: When you encounter Scripture, search for at least one application of it. For example, when reading

God's Word, say to yourself, "I won't close my Bible until I can prayerfully think of at least one way to apply what I've read." Such mental scouring of the Scripture for an application *is* meditation, or at least one form of it.

So as you reflect on the text, do you perceive something God would have you . . .

- Stop?
- Start?
- Believe?
- Confess?
- Pray about?
- Thank Him for?
- Communicate to someone?

We cannot expect the Bible to advance our transformation without meditation and application.

ASK THE PHILIPPIANS 4:8 QUESTIONS

WHEN MEDITATING ON A VERSE OF SCRIPTURE, IT'S USUALLY MUCH easier to answer specific questions about it than to think about the text without any guidance or direction at all.

Recently, I was meditating on Philippians 4:8: "Finally, brethren, whatever things are true, whatever things are noble, whatever things are just, whatever things are pure, whatever things are lovely, whatever things are of good report, if there is any virtue and if there is anything praiseworthy—meditate on these things." It occurred to me that the directions given here for the kinds of things we should meditate on could serve as a list of things to look for in any verse I consider. As a result (and after consulting several translations of Philippians 4:8), I developed a series of questions based upon these things.

But while much of our meditation begins with Scripture and then applies it to life, it is also valid to begin by meditating on something in your life and then taking that to Scripture. You might reflect, for example, on the possible reasons God allowed something to happen to you, but then ultimately submit your thoughts to the sound foundation of Scripture, such as a text like Psalm 31:14-15.

In either case, that is, whether meditating on something in your life—an event, an experience, an encounter with someone, even a part of creation—or whether meditating on a verse or story in the Bible, the Philippians 4:8 questions can be a helpful guide. In fact, when thinking about *anything*, try asking:

- What is *true* about this, or what truth does it exemplify?
- What is *honorable* about this?
- What is *right* about this?

- What is *pure* about this, or how does it exemplify purity?
- What is *lovely* about this?
- What is *admirable*, *commendable*, or *reputation-strengthening* about this?
- What is *excellent* about this (in other words, excels others of this kind)?
- What is *praiseworthy* about this?

Ask the Joseph Hall Questions

Joseph Hall (1574–1656) was an Anglican bishop in Norwich, England. McClintock and Strong's religious encyclopedia describes him as a "man of very devotional habits," observing that "intense was his ardor in the pursuit of intellectual and spiritual improvement." Hall's 1607 book, *The Art of Divine Meditation,* was one of the most influential books of its day. In this Puritan devotional classic he discussed and illustrated the use of ten questions helpful in meditating on Scripture. A twentieth-century writer[2] asserted that Hall's questions were already well known to ministers by the time *The Art of Divine Meditation* popularized them, noting that a similar form of them was published more than fifty years earlier.[3]

I find meditation on Scripture simpler, and yet more fruitful when guided by Hall's questions. I have modified and expanded them slightly to make them clearer to contemporary readers.

1. What is it (*define and/or describe* what it is) you are meditating upon?
2. What are its *divisions* or *parts*?
3. What *causes* it?
4. What does it *cause*, that is, what are its *fruits and effects*?
5. What is its *place, location,* or *use*?
6. What are its *qualities* and *attachments*?
7. What is *contrary to, contradictory of,* or *different* from it?
8. What *compares* to it?
9. What are its *titles* or *names*?
10. What are the *testimonies* or *examples of Scripture* about it?

The first question is the most important, for the answer becomes the "it" referred to in the rest of the questions. So if the verse you were meditating upon were, say, Romans 8:28, your answer to question 1 might be something like, "God's control of all things for the good of His people." Then its divisions or parts (question 2) would include "God's control," "all things," and "His people."

You might find it useful to keep a copy of these questions in your Bible, planner, computer, or on your desk.

By asking these brief questions, countless believers since the days of the English Puritans have generated enormous amounts of valuable insights into the texts they meditated upon. So can you.

SIMPLIFYING AND PRAYER

Ask, and You Will Receive
Something Good

One way to simplify your prayer life is simply to ask. Perhaps more often than we realize, we want God to do something for us or to give something to us, and yet we haven't actually asked Him for it. "You do not have," says James 4:2, "because you do not ask." The failure to ask is not the only reason we do not have, for the Bible has many other things to say about what we should ask for and why we should ask. In fact, in the very next verse we read, "You ask and do not receive, because you ask amiss, that you may spend it on your pleasures" (verse 3).

Even so, Jesus made some remarkable promises about simply asking of God in prayer. In the Sermon on the Mount, He assured, "Ask, and it will be given to you; seek, and you will find; knock, and it will be opened to you. For everyone who asks receives, and he who seeks finds, and to him who knocks it will be opened" (Matthew 7:7-8).

While any passage on prayer needs to be placed in the context of the entire Bible's teaching on the subject, it's easy to add so many biblical qualifiers to this broad promise that we end up doubting it more than believing it. But rather than discourage us from asking, Jesus emphasized three times what "will" result from asking, seeking, and knocking at the door of Heaven. Then to further embolden us, He promises that *"everyone* who asks receives" (emphasis added).

Of course, we may not receive exactly what we ask for. (And I thank God for this when I remember some of the things I've requested.) But we *will* receive something good. For Jesus continued, "Or what man is there among you who, if his son asks for bread, will give him a stone? Or if he asks for a fish, will he give him a serpent? If you then, being evil, know how to give good gifts to your children, how much more will your Father who is in heaven give good things to those who ask Him!" (verses 9-11).

Because God is good, He will give "good things" to all who ask Him. We do not know what they are or when He will give them, for the good things given in answer to many prayers will be seen only in Heaven. But Jesus said, "Ask." Simply ask, and you will receive something good.

DON'T ALWAYS PRAY THE SAME PRAYER

SOME PEOPLE ALWAYS PRAY THE SAME PRAYER, WHETHER THEY PRAY IT just once a day or repeat it many times. They may use words straight out of Scripture, even praying one of the prayers of the Bible word for word, or they may speak sentences of a merely human origin. Either way, in Heaven their prayers must sound like an unchanging voicemail recording.

But one prayer does not a prayer life make. Prayers without variety eventually become words without meaning. Jesus said that to pray this way is to pray in vain, for in the Sermon on the Mount, He warned, "And when you pray, do not use vain repetitions as the heathen do. For they think that they will be heard for their many words" (Matthew 6:7).

What, then, about Jesus' teaching in the Lord's Prayer? Don't His introductory words to the prayer in Luke 11:2, "When you pray, say . . . ," indicate that He wants us to repeat the words of this prayer verbatim? And if so, how can doing this involve "vain repetitions" since these are inspired words Jesus specifically told us to pray?

While it's true that this command of Jesus in Luke 11:2 justifies praying the exact words of the prayer, remember that when He taught this prayer to His hearers in Matthew 6:9, He began by saying, "In this *manner,* therefore, pray" (emphasis added). That's why, even though the prayer has been recited in unison by worshipers since the second century, it has been called the "Model" Prayer, because in it Jesus models all the elements we should include in our prayers. Not even the apostles understood the Lord's words here to be the exact and only words we're to use in prayer, for we never read in the New Testament of the apostles repeating them nor of their teaching others to do so. The other prayers of the New Testament follow the *model* of this prayer, but not its *form*. Any prayer in the Bible consistent with the Model Prayer may also be prayed sincerely and/or used as a model, but none should be considered merely a script to be repeated ritualistically.

Jesus also taught the importance of perseverance in prayer (see Matthew 7:7-8; Luke 18:1-8), meaning that it's often necessary to pray many times (maybe even for years) for the same thing. But frequent prayer for the same thing is very different from vain repetition of the same prayer. We should never think that we have found "just the right words" and make them the sum total of our prayer life.

It may seem simpler to pray only one prayer all the time rather than learning to pray in accordance with all that the Bible teaches on prayer. But in reality, such praying is an *over*simplification that reduces prayer to a magic formula designed to get God to do our bidding. The entire Bible is our guide to prayer and to willfully neglect what God says about it throughout Scripture in order to isolate our attention on one prayer is a waste of breath.

Besides, talking to God is too great a privilege to settle for "vain repetitions" when the Bible invites you to "pour out your heart before Him" (Psalm 62:8).

Pray Scripture

"VAIN REPETITIONS" ARE RUINOUS IN ANY AREA OF SPIRITUALITY, BUT especially in prayer. Jesus warned, "And when you pray, do not use vain repetitions as the heathen do. For they think that they will be heard for their many words" (Matthew 6:7). One of the reasons Jesus prohibited the empty repetition of prayers is because that's exactly the way we're prone to pray. Although I don't merely recite memorized prayers, my own tendency is to pray basically the same old things about the same old things. And it doesn't take long before this fragments the attention span and freezes the heart of prayer. The problem is not our praying *about* the same old things, for Jesus taught us (in Luke 11:5-13; 18:1-8) to pray with persistence for good things. Our problem is in always praying about them with the same ritualistic, heartless expressions.

In my experience, the almost unfailing solution to this problem is to pray through a passage of Scripture—particularly one of the psalms—instead of making up my prayer as I go. Praying in this way is simply taking the words of Scripture and using them as my own words or as prompters for what I say to God.

For example, if I were praying through Psalm 27, I would begin by reading verse 1: "The LORD is my light and my salvation." Then I would pray something like, "Thank You, Lord, that You are my light. Thank You for giving me the light to see my need for Jesus and Your forgiveness. Please light my way so that I will know which way to go in the big decision that is before me today. And thank You especially that You are my salvation. You saved me; I didn't save myself. And now I ask You to save my children also, as well as those at work with whom I've shared the gospel."

When I have nothing else to say, instead of my mind wandering, I have a place to go—the rest of verse 1: "Of whom shall I be afraid?" Then I might pray along these lines: "I thank You that I do not have to fear anyone because You are my Father. But I confess that I have been fearful about _____." I would continue in this way, praying about whatever is prompted verse by verse, until I either complete the psalm or run out of time.

Praying through a passage of Scripture was the uncomplicated method that transformed the daily experience of one of the most famous men of prayer in history. George Müller said,

> Formerly when I rose, I began to pray as soon as possible, and generally spent all my time till breakfast in prayer. . . . What was the result? . . . Often, after having suffered much from wandering of mind for the first ten minutes, or quarter of an hour, or even half an hour, I only then began really to pray.
>
> I scarcely ever suffer now in this way. For my heart being nourished by the truth, being brought into experimental [that is, experiential] fellowship with God, I speak to my Father . . . about the things that He has brought before me in His precious Word.[1]

Both Jesus (in Matthew 27:46) and His followers in the book of Acts (4:24-26) prayed words from the Psalms (from Psalm 22:1, and Psalm 146:6 and Psalm 2:1-2 respectively). Why not you? Although you'll pray about "the same old things," you'll do so in brand-new ways. You'll also find yourself praying about things you never thought to—things that are on the heart of God. You'll concentrate better, and begin to experience prayer as a real conversation with a real Person. For the Bible really *is* God speaking to you, and now all you have to do is simply respond to what He says.

Pray the Prayers of Others

READING THE WRITTEN PRAYERS OF OTHERS USUALLY WEARIES ME. I've read several books containing the compiled prayers of one or several godly believers, and while occasionally one of the prayers stirs my heart, generally they don't energize my praying.

An exception, however, is *The Valley of Vision: A Collection of Puritan Prayers and Devotions.*[2] With one exception, I've given away more copies of this book than any other. The reason I find it so helpful is that the editor of this volume researched a number of albums of prayers (and despite the subtitle, they weren't all from Puritans) and selected the best from them for *The Valley of Vision.*

For instance, (and such brief excerpts cannot accurately reflect the beauty and feeling of the page-long prayers):

My Father,
Enlarge my heart, warm my affections, open my lips,
    supply words that proclaim "Love lustres at Calvary."
There grace removes my burdens and heaps them on thy Son,
    made a transgressor, a curse, and sin for me. . . .
My Saviour wept that all tears might be wiped from my eyes,
    groaned that I might have endless song,
    endured all pain that I might have unfading health,
    bore a thorned crown that I might have a glory-diadem,
    bowed his head that I might uplift mine,
    experienced reproach that I might receive welcome,
    closed his eyes in death that I might gaze on unclouded
    brightness,
    expired that I might for ever live.

O Father, who spared not thine only Son that thou mightest spare me . . .
Help me to adore thee by lips and life.[3]

And again:

Lord, high and holy, meek and lowly,
Thou hast brought me to the valley of vision,
 where I live in the depths but see thee in the heights;
 hemmed in by mountains of sin I behold thy glory.
Let me learn by paradox
 that the way down is the way up,
 that to be low is to be high,
 that the broken heart is the healed heart,
 that the contrite spirit is the rejoicing spirit,
 that the repenting soul is the victorious soul,
 that to have nothing is to possess all,
 that to bear the cross is to wear the crown,
 that to give is to receive,
 that the valley is the place of vision.
Lord, in the daytime stars can be seen from deepest wells,
 and the deeper the wells the brighter thy stars shine;
Let me find thy light in my darkness,
 thy life in my death,
 thy joy in my sorrow,
 thy grace in my sin,
 thy riches in my poverty,
 thy glory in my valley.[4]

The method is not merely to repeat these lines as though they were magic words. Rather, they are designed to ignite the heart and mind in Godward blazes, to be fiery phrases caught up in the flames of your own words. When there's a spiritual chill in your own expressions, try praying the prayers of others.

Take a Prayer Walk

One of the most common struggles in the practice of spirituality is maintaining mental focus in prayer. When I try to pray, I often find myself thinking about my to-do list or daydreaming instead of talking to God. But walking as I pray—either in a large place indoors (such as a church building), or more frequently, outdoors—usually keeps my mind from wandering as easily. In addition, I typically bring a small Bible to prompt my prayer periodically during the walk.

The walking and the weather invigorate my sluggish soul. Looking up into the blue or out to the horizon refreshes my sense of the greatness of God. The sights, smells, and sounds of my Father's world surround me with reminders of His presence. The cadence of my pace, or occasionally stopping to stare into the distance, often enables me to concentrate in prayer more easily than when I'm still and my eyes are closed.

Abraham's son Isaac is an example from Scripture of walking while thinking on the things of God. Genesis 24:63 reports, "And Isaac went out to meditate in the field." Four hundred years ago, an English Puritan named Joseph Hall wrote in his influential book *The Art of Divine Meditation,* "All our teachers of meditation have commended various positions of the body, according to their own disposition and practice. . . . But of all others, I think that Isaac's choice was best, who meditated walking."[5]

Perhaps no one in church history is more closely associated with a life of meditative prayer than George Müller. He lived during the nineteenth century in Bristol, England, where he founded an orphanage and a literature distribution ministry. Müller recorded more than fifty thousand specific answers to prayer, thirty thousand of which he said were answered the same day he prayed. Notice that his normal mode of prayer was a meditative prayer walk:

> I find it very beneficial to my health to walk thus for meditation before breakfast, and . . . generally take out a New Testament . . . and I find that I can profitably spend my time in the open air.
>
> I used to consider the time spent in walking a loss, but now I find it very profitable, not only to my body, but also to my soul. . . . For . . . I speak to my Father . . . about the things that He has brought before me in His precious Word.[6]

Simplify the struggle of staying focused in prayer, and refresh both body and soul with a leisurely walk in conversation with God from His Word.

Pray Without Filler

"And Father, we, um, just want to thank You for Your blessings. And, uh, we just, Lord, want to, uh, just thank You, Lord, for just, really just being so good to us, Father. And Father, we just ask that You just forgive us of our sins, Father. And, um, just bless us now, Father, and just lead, guide, and direct us, Lord. And we just ask all this in Jesus' name, Father, amen."

Although there are several problems with praying such soul-deadening prayers, I want to point out two. Both have to do with using words purposelessly.

First, recall that in the Third Commandment, God tells us, "You shall not take the name of the LORD your God in vain, for the LORD will not hold him guiltless who takes His name in vain" (Exodus 20:7). The original Hebrew here means that we should not use the Lord's name emptily or without purpose. When we use God's name like filler for our prayers, or when we address Him again and again without any real purpose in doing so, we take His name in vain.

Second, repeatedly using the name of the Lord or "um," "uh," "just," and the like, typically reflects thoughtless prayer. The person launches out into prayer, but drifts aimlessly from one random thought to another. He's "just praying," and not praying about much of anything in particular. This pattern tends toward heartless prayer as well. The words sound hollow. They convey no sense of urgency or importance about the prayer. And if our prayers do not even move us, how do we expect them to move God? None of the prayers in the Bible sound so pointless or flat. Instead we read of men like Elijah who "prayed earnestly" (James 5:17).

Removing needless and meaningless verbal filler makes our prayers clearer, stronger, and more like a purposeful conversation with God.

HAVE A REAL PRAYER CLOSET

AS I SIT WRITING THESE WORDS WITH MY OLD SWAN FOUNTAIN PEN on an oak roll-top desk, my left forearm rests on a book called *Writers' Houses.*[7] On end in a cubbyhole to my right is another book of photographs called *The Writer's Desk.*[8] As a writer, I enjoy looking at pictures of the private places where famous authors practiced their craft.

We expect a writer to dedicate a room in his home for writing, or a musician to set aside space in her residence just for music, or an artist to use one of the rooms where he lives as a studio. Many people do all or part of their daily work from offices at home. Why, then, shouldn't a Christian have a place in the house devoted exclusively to the work of prayer?

In the Sermon on the Mount, Jesus spoke of how hypocrites love to pray so that people can see or hear them and be impressed. "But you," He instructed, "when you pray, go into your room, and when you have shut your door, pray to your Father who is in the secret place; and your Father who sees in secret will reward you openly" (Matthew 6:6).

In the King James Version of the Bible, the word translated here as *room* is rendered *closet,* giving rise to a now old-fashioned term, "prayer closet." While the Lord's primary emphasis in this verse is on the importance of sincere, humble, private prayer, why *not* have a place—a prayer closet—in your home set aside just for meeting with God?

While it's true that many will not have the space to dedicate an area entirely for prayer, what does it say about the priorities of Christians who have a whole room for physical exercise, but no place only for spiritual exercises? What does it say when we allocate a large space just for children to play, but none for Christians to pray? What does it say when we design the most spacious area in the home for our entertainment, filling it with a large TV, music system, and computer whereby we hear from the world, but make no plans for a place where we meet with God?

It's not that we can't use a desk both for work and prayer, or that we can't read the Bible in the same chair where we watch TV. But why shouldn't the home of a Christian demonstrate by design — whether a small room or a renovated closet — that prayer to God is important?

Pray Through Today's Plans

Have you realized that planning your day can be a part of your devotional life? The wise counsel of Proverbs 16:3 says, "Commit your works to the LORD, and your thoughts will be established." The "thoughts" spoken of here is a term often rendered "plans" in other translations. Your "thoughts" about the day before you generally include your "plans" for the day. These plans, according to this verse, "will be established" only as you "commit your works to the LORD."

Moreover, the rest of the Bible teaches us that we can't expect our plans to be established if they or our works are contrary to the Lord's will. But this verse states another link between our plans and our works that execute those plans: We should commit our works to the Lord.

The Hebrew word here translated *commit* means "to roll," as in to roll one's burdens on the Lord. The same word is used at the beginning of Psalm 37:5: "Commit your way to the LORD, trust also in Him, and He shall bring it to pass."

How do we do this? "This would be accomplished with a spirit of humility and by means of a diligent season of prayer," says one Old Testament scholar.[9]

One way I often try to flesh this out is to take my to-do list for the day and write a generous estimate beside each activity of how long I expect it to take. In light of my fixed commitments, usually I see that there aren't enough hours in the day to accomplish everything on the list. But it's always better for me to realize this in advance than to discover it in frustration toward the end of the day. Then I can look prayerfully over the list to determine which items get priority and which must be moved to tomorrow's list. I commit the remaining items on the list to the Lord, asking for His guidance and blessing.

Rolling each anticipated event of the day upon the Lord simplifies my spiritual life by integrating my spirituality with daily living. Instead of segmenting the things of God from "real life," or perceiving my devotional life as merely another part of my day, I look to Him regarding my entire day. And doing this at the outset usually results in a greater God-consciousness in the midst of the details and ordinary activities of the day as well.

To begin my day without any sense of the Lord's will regarding my plans, or to begin my works without committing them to the Lord, reflects the same kind of independence that brought sin into the world. By contrast, dependence on God is at the heart of true spirituality. As Jesus was often found beginning His day in dependent prayer, and as acceptance with God comes only through dependence upon the work of Jesus on our behalf, so there is wisdom in a conscious, Godward look of dependence about the details of life this day.

USE PRAYER PROMPTS

BESIDE A HIGHWAY THAT I TRAVEL SEVERAL TIMES EACH WEEK SITS A big sign that's hard to ignore. Whenever I notice it, I use it as a reminder to pray for a particular person. At another point along that road is a panoramic view of my city. I use the sight to remind me to ask the Lord for reformation and revival upon His work in our area. Whenever I see a certain time on a digital clock, it's a memory-jogger to pray for my wife and daughter.

I refer to these as "prayer prompts," things I use to remind me to pray for specific people or situations.

Christians have always used commonplace things as ways to turn their thoughts heavenward. When dressing in the morning, many Puritans made a habit of praying briefly for a different matter with each article of clothing they pulled on. I know several believers who pray whenever they hear a siren.

All this is similar to a practice of the apostle Paul. Every time the thought of the church in Philippi popped into his head, he used that recollection as a reminder to pray for those brothers and sisters: "I thank my God upon every remembrance of you, always in every prayer of mine making request for you all with joy" (Philippians 1:3-4).

Why not transform something from your routine into a prayer prompt? It can be a sight, smell, sound, thought, event, or experience. Find these cues in your home, at your job, on your commute, online, at your desk — anywhere.

Whenever you get up in the night you could pray for the salvation of your family. While brushing your teeth (you have to think about something!) you could intercede for your church. Every time you see or hear a particular commercial (perhaps one that's especially annoying) on TV, radio, or the Internet, you could pray for unreached people groups. Certain billboards could prompt you to ask God to bring an end to abortion. Each email from a given source might serve as your cue to pray for your own faithfulness to the Lord.

I'm not suggesting that these would be the only times you pray for these matters. Instead, these prayer prompts could supply frequent reminders to pray *additionally* for things that are of special or ongoing importance.

Transform something mundane, even something negative, into something that will turn your thoughts to God.

SIMPLIFYING
AND
YOUR
JOURNAL

Keep a Simple Journal

Do you know the first names of any of your great-grandparents? Unless one of your hobbies is genealogy, the answer is probably no. And yet they lived lives as full as ours. They went to school, married, and had children. Most of them worked at their various occupations for decades and played with infants who grew to become your parents. In all likelihood, your great-grandparents were very much alive less than one hundred years ago. But after all their labors and all the seasons they saw come and go, what awareness is there now that they ever drew a breath? If you, the direct descendant of these eight people, do not even know their names, then it's almost certain that no one else knows them or anything else about them either. They may have lived for eighty years, and not a trace of their lives remains.

That's *your* life in less than one hundred years from today.

Despite the length of your life, all your hard work, all you've accumulated, and all you've done for and with your children and grandchildren, it's unlikely that anyone will know anything about you in less than a thousand months from now—except for what you write.

To leave a trace of your life—that's only one of many reasons to keep a journal. The people of God have kept written records of the works and ways of God in their lives since Bible times. The Bible itself contains some God-inspired journals. Many psalms are pages from the heart of King David's personal spiritual journey with the Lord. The journal of the prophet Jeremiah's feelings about the fall of Jerusalem we call the book of Lamentations.

Keeping a journal can be one of the most profitable and fruitful spiritual disciplines we ever practice. Among other things, it helps in self-understanding and evaluation, in meditating on the Lord and His Word, in expressing our deepest feelings to the Lord and in remembering His works in our lives. Journaling assists in creating and preserving a spiritual heritage, in clarifying and articulating insights and impressions, in monitoring goals and priorities, and in maintaining the other spiritual disciplines.[1] Besides the profit it brings to our spiritual health, recent medical studies indicate that journal keeping can even benefit our physical health.

However, some people imagine journaling to be more complicated than it is. In fact, it's quite simple. Just write. Unlike some of the other spiritual disciplines, there's no right or wrong way to keep a journal. The journal entries of some folks consist primarily of their reflections about events of the day. For others, meditations on Scripture dominate their pages. Still others fill the lines with prayers, poems, or a random combination of all the above.

Nothing says you have to write every day or that you must include a certain number of lines. Journals can be handwritten, computer-generated, or even audio- or video-recorded.

The simplest way is best. It's the one you're most likely to maintain over a lifetime to build a monument to God's faithfulness. And long after you've made your last entry, it's also the one most likely to introduce your great-grandchildren to your life and faith and to influence them for Christ's sake.

Practice Random Acts of Journaling

PROBABLY THE MOST COMMON TYPES OF JOURNAL ENTRIES BY Christians are reflections on daily events and meditations on Scripture. Besides these, occasionally you might include some of the following random ideas:

- Prayers
- Sermon notes
- Letters you want to write, but will not or cannot send
- Mind maps (read *The Mind Map Book* by Tony Buzan[2] and use his technique to put your thoughts—especially your meditations on Scripture—in your journal)
- Quotations from books, sermons, friends, teachers, and the like
- Interactions with your reading (perhaps even a kind of book review)
- Thought-provoking questions
- Poetry
- Important early memories you should preserve
- Annual list of books read (on your own or to your family)

In addition to these ideas of things to put in your journal, here are five suggestions to make your journal keeping more fruitful.

- When you don't have the time or the heart to journal, write just one sentence. As you do, you'll almost always decide to write a little more. But even if you write only one line, those few words will help preserve the presence of this spiritual discipline in your life.
- Print extra copies (or photocopy your handwritten entries)

and place them in the appropriate biblical or topical files. For instance, if you meditate on John 3:16, place a copy in a file labeled "John" or in another where you keep Bible-related material. And/or you might place a copy in a file "God's love." Then when you next study or teach on John 3:16 or on the love of God, you'll quickly find the fruit of your meditation.

- Index your journal. Indexing enables you to find and use your entries years later. Some give titles to each entry ("Car Trouble") or simply note the themes ("Church" or "Work"), sometimes in the margin. If your journal is in your computer, use the indexing feature of your word processor. We're thankful today that the brilliant minister Jonathan Edwards indexed his *Miscellanies*. He numbered each entry, and then elsewhere recorded the numbers under alphabetized headings. The number of entry 287, for example, might be written under both "Sin" and "Salvation" if it pertained to both. Edwards also indexed every Bible verse mentioned in his journal. In this way he could quickly locate all his written thoughts about any subject or verse.

- Write quickly. While journaling should often (almost always?) be a leisurely, reflective experience, sometimes writing quickly enables you to say what you *really* think more freely. For this reason, writing coaches often recommend fast, uncensored writing for things like warm-ups, first drafts, and journal entries. You'll more likely write what's in your heart when you aren't simultaneously concerned about grammar or style.

- Begin with, "What I really want to say is . . . " Sometimes this helps to get right to the point and express your true feelings.

Whether you are a diligent journal keeper or someone about to start, remember that the ultimate purpose for this and all the other spiritual disciplines is "for the purpose of godliness" (1 Timothy 4:7, NASB).

PROBE YOUR SOUL WITH QUESTIONS

GEORGE WHITEFIELD (1714–1770) WAS "THE BEST-KNOWN EVAN-gelist of the eighteenth century and one of the greatest itinerant preachers in the history of Protestantism."[3] Before he retired each night, he opened his journal and probed his soul with questions such as these he'd placed in the flyleaf:

Have I,

1. Been fervent in prayer?
2. After or before every deliberate conversation or action, considered how it might tend to God's glory?
3. After any pleasure, immediately given thanks?
4. Planned business for the day?
5. Been simple and recollected in everything?
6. Been meek, cheerful, affable in everything I said or did?
7. Been proud, vain, unchaste, or enviable of others?
8. Recollected in eating and drinking? Thankful? Temperate in sleep?
9. Thought or spoken unkindly of anyone?
10. Confessed all sins?[4]

A more famous contemporary of Whitefield's, Jonathan Edwards, compiled a list of resolutions that is still widely circulated. Posted in his journal for frequent review, they were his lifelong spiritual goals and priorities. What isn't as well known about these resolutions is that Edwards regularly evaluated himself against them and recorded the results in his journal.[5]

Due in no small part to these continual, soul-searching inquiries, Whitefield and Edwards became increasingly conformed to Christlikeness in life and character.

While I heartily recommend this practice of Whitefield and Edwards (and of countless others throughout church history), there are other ways to use questions like these. For instance, in addition to your individual spirituality you could also ask yourself specifically about your marriage and family life, work, Internet habits, financial stewardship, or any other area of life where frequent reminders to obedience would help. Several years ago, I used a similar method not only to remind myself of previous commitments, but also to cultivate some new habits as well. If you develop a long list of questions, you might review a small number daily rather than the entire list.

The Bible directs each of us to "examine himself" before taking the Lord's Supper (1 Corinthians 11:28). Similarly, 2 Corinthians 13:5 instructs us, "Examine yourselves as to whether you are in the faith. Test yourselves." Using an established series of soul-probing questions can simplify the ongoing process of obedience to such commands and make it easier for us to keep short accounts with God.

Use Journal Prompts, Part 1

I SUPPOSE THAT IF THE TERM "WRITER'S BLOCK" APPLIES TO JOURNAL keeping, then that was my problem. There's always something to write about, but because mine is primarily a spiritual journal, I wanted to write about something that would edify my soul. On that day, however, no particular subject emerged from my mental fog.

It's not that I won't write about general subjects, for I do. I just want to discipline myself to write as much as possible about matters that relate directly to the spiritual life. Besides, Philippians 4:8 tells me, "Finally, brethren, whatever things are true, whatever things are noble, whatever things are just, whatever things are pure, whatever things are lovely, whatever things are of good report, if there is any virtue and if there is anything praiseworthy—meditate on these things." So I want to meditate on and journal about "these things" whenever I can.

The idea occurred to me to make a list of thirty-one subjects (one for each day of the month) that relate to my spiritual life. And if, for example, on the eighteenth of the month I don't know what to journal about, I can turn to my "journal prompts," look for number 18, and follow its prompting to write about fellowship. As a result, I might write about my need for fellowship, a specific way I can initiate fellowship with someone the next time I'm at church, how technology affects fellowship, a recent experience of fellowship, or something else prompted by the word.

While certainly not unchangeable, here is the list I quickly composed:

1. Love for God
2. Love for others
3. Evangelism
4. Bible intake
5. Meditation on Scripture
6. Application of Scripture
7. Prayer
8. Worship (public or private)
9. Serving
10. Stewardship of time
11. Stewardship of money
12. Fasting
13. Silence and Solitude
14. Journaling
15. Learning/mind
16. Persevering
17. The Lord's Day
18. Fellowship
19. The tongue
20. Thought life
21. Family
22. Ministry
23. Joy
24. Simplifying
25. Body
26. Faith
27. Reformation
28. Revival
29. Cross
30. Sin
31. Last things (death, judgment, Heaven, Hell)

Sometimes the simplicity of a predetermined subject can make it easier to maintain the discipline of journal keeping.

Use Journal Prompts, Part 2

Journal prompts are thought-starters to use when you draw a blank about what to write in your spiritual journal. In the previous chapter I suggested a list of thirty-one subjects, so that on any given day you have a prompt that corresponds with the day of the month. So on the seventh of the month, if you need an idea of something to write about, journal prompt number 7 suggests that you write about prayer. The stewardship of your time is the theme to consider on the tenth. And if you can't think of anything on the twenty-third, joy is the proposed topic.

Another method involves the use of specific questions. The questions should apply to every day of the year and stimulate thoughtful entries. Ideally, each question should provoke enough response that only one or two would suffice as a day's entry.

Try these ten questions. (If you write in your journal at the beginning of your day, you would replace the word *today* with *yesterday*, and *tomorrow* with *today*.)

1. What was the most important thing that happened today?
2. What did I learn today?
3. Where did I see God at work today?
4. What was the most significant thing someone said to me today?
5. When was I most aware of the Lord today?
6. What was the most helpful thing I read today?
7. What should I have done differently today?
8. How can I simplify my life tomorrow?
9. What could I do to glorify God the most tomorrow?
10. What difference can I make in someone's life tomorrow?

The Bible says, "Let each one examine his own work" (Galatians 6:4). One simple and practical way to do this is to use questions like these on occasion as journal prompts.

Journal with a Fountain Pen

I enjoy writing in my journal with a fountain pen. Yes, an old-fashioned fountain pen. And whether a new model or a vintage pen, with a stiff nib or a flexible one, a good fountain pen is a pleasure to write with. Even the ritual of pausing to draw ink from a bottle into a thirsty pen can bring a sense of nostalgic satisfaction in our high-tech, efficiency-driven world. I commend this method of journal writing to you.

Journaling with a pen adds variety to this discipline, a change from always clacking entries into a computer. In some cases, writing by hand affords a flexibility of time and place for journaling that electronic means cannot allow. The variation in method or location may even spark more creative entries, for fresh ideas often follow fresh approaches.

There's also an intentional slowness to journaling with a fountain pen. When I'm dancing all ten fingers as rapidly as possible in front of my computer, it's hard for my soul to be serene. But watching my words take shape with the free flow of ink to paper frequently helps my soul decelerate to the pace of my body.

What's more, there can be a beauty in the strokes of a pen that goes beyond the strict utility of just recording your thoughts. Writing by hand with a splendid pen is more expressive than banging out words on a plastic keyboard. Despite all it can do, the computer cannot replace the singular quality that has caused the fountain pen to endure for generations. Even the pen itself can be beautiful, something we don't typically ascribe to computers.

"But my handwriting's awful," you say. A fountain pen immediately improves it, sometimes dramatically. Using a good pen in a meditative frame of mind also causes you to take more time with the turn of the letters, adding flourishes and style that beautify your script.

I don't say that you should always use a pen when journaling. If I know I'm likely to write several pages, I'll almost always choose the computer because of time constraints. And there are times when, as I've advocated elsewhere, it frees the heart or the thought flow to write in your journal quickly. But you can do that with a pen, and not just with a computer.

No matter whether you put your thoughts on paper with a fountain pen or a computer, use an acid-free paper that will last. Many standard copier/printer papers are acid-free. They can also work for handwritten entries. I cut sheets in half and hole-punch them to fit in my ring-binder journal. Be aware that a fountain pen works differently on different papers. On some coarse papers, like those found in some handsomely bound journals, the ink can bleed.

As with any discipline, journaling can become routine, so use tools that will invite you to write. If necessary, ask a fountain pen user or at a pen shop about pens and papers. You might even find a colorful ink that makes you want to fill a page. Depending upon the pen, you may not have to use bottled ink unless you choose to do so. Many pens can use either cartridges (convenient for traveling) or bottled ink.

Finally, there's a simplicity inherent in using a pen to write in a journal. It doesn't require electronics, a printer, or batteries. It can slow us into the same mental rhythms of the one who penned, "This will be written for the generation to come, that a people yet to be created may praise the LORD" (Psalm 102:18), and of the apostle Paul, who dipped a quill to say, "I have written to you with my own hand" (Galatians 6:11).

The heft of a pen in my hand with the things of God on my mind has often been good for my soul. Try it for yours.

SIMPLIFYING
AND
YOUR
MIND

Avoid Spiritual Anesthesia

Television is the most powerful cultural influence on the planet, but it does little to promote either simplicity or biblical spirituality. Instead, like spiritual anesthesia, TV dulls the sensitivity of the soul.

For instance, almost any show you see will laugh at something God says is good or normalize something God calls sin (see Isaiah 5:20). Television frequently contradicts God, almost as directly as the serpent in the Garden of Eden (see Genesis 3:4). It saturates the mind of the viewer with the world's way of thinking. Television displays a rapid succession of pictures that we passively observe (in contrast to forming mental pictures ourselves, as when reading), which causes the imagination to atrophy with inactivity. And this makes the concentration and meditation on Scripture more difficult. On top of everything else, watching TV simply takes time, time that we later say we don't have for our spiritual disciplines. Other than (possibly) a very few obscure Christian broadcasts, where on TV can you find a good example of what you want to be spiritually?

Beyond its impact on our spirituality, TV is no friend of anyone trying to simplify, either. In fact, TV's very existence depends upon an incessant parade of advertising intended to make us feel discontented with our experiences, possessions, relationships, and appearance. In the words of writer Wendell Berry, TV persuades us to believe "that all worth experiencing is somewhere else and that all worth having must be bought."[1]

I cannot pronounce God's complete will for you regarding TV. But as you seek Him on what is good for your soul in this matter, remember James 4:17: "Therefore, to him who knows to do good and does not do it, to him it is sin." Television may not have the power to kill the Christian soul, but it anesthetizes it by the hour. Wake up!

Turn It Off!

When my mother's parents married on March 29, 1919, they moved into a small house near a community outside Tupelo, Mississippi. Their home had no electricity, telephone, or radio. It was quiet.

After my grandfather went to the fields in the morning, the only sounds he heard all day were those of God's creation or the ones he himself made—the crunch of the plow in the ground, his cries of "Gee" or "Haw" to the mules, and his singing. Back in the farmhouse, the only sounds my grandmother heard were the ones she made while working around the house, or the sounds of God's creation—the birds, the wind—that came through the open windows. They were alone with their thoughts and their God all day long.

If my grandparents wanted information, conversation, or music, they had to make a special effort, hitching up the team and taking a long ride in an open, bumpy wagon. Mostly, this happened on Saturday when they did their weekly business—"trading" they called it—in town. The majority of the music they heard was in church.

Our experience is just the opposite. Friends or families go out to eat together and their conversation is distracted by loud music and TVs in every corner. Children riding in a vehicle watch TV or listen to music on their headphones, while their parents listen to something else on the radio. It's hard to go anyplace void of music, TV, or personal messages mediated by technology. Portable electronics allow us to perpetually surround ourselves with sound. Whereas my grandparents had to make an effort to break the silence and hear news or music, we have to make an effort to avoid information and entertainment. And sometimes we need to—for the health of our souls.

So turn off the radio in the car for a day or two. Sit outside after dinner and talk or read. Spend an evening by the fire without the TV. Recover the physically and spiritually re-creative power of silence.

READ ONE PAGE PER DAY

WHEN LIFE GETS TOO COMPLEX, ONE OF THE FIRST PARTS OF A healthy spiritual life to decline is reading. I talk to well-intentioned Christians almost every week who confess to growing piles of books by their "reading chair," desk, nightstand, and other places, but who never have time to read. Reading for sheer enjoyment was long ago forsaken. Reading for Christian growth rarely happens. Most days, a few minutes in the Bible is all that's left of their reading. Those who love to learn and those who want to grow grieve the loss of reading like the loss of a close friend. "But what can I do?" they sigh. "There are only so many hours in a day."

To these overwhelmed believers I usually ask, "Do you think you could find the time to read one page of a book each day?" No one has ever told me they couldn't, no matter how busy they are or how many children they have. It might mean sneaking a page during a visit to the bathroom, sitting in the car an extra two minutes at the end of the morning or evening commute, or standing by the bed to read a moment before crashing into the pillow at night.

By reading one page per day you can read 365 pages in a year, or the equivalent of two full-length books. That may not sound like much, but it's far better than not reading at all. Moreover, by some accounts this would place you above half the U.S. population in the number of books read each year.

Furthermore, if you read just two books a year for the rest of your life, think of how many books you'd read if you lived to be seventy or seventy-five. Add to these all the books you might read in your retirement years if you develop the habit of reading just a little each day now.

By this means of just a page per day, I've seen mothers of multiple preschoolers, homeschooling moms, and overwhelmed executives alike plow through a book every month or two. It wasn't because they had any less to do. Rather, the secret lay in the simple discipline of making the commitment to read just one page. Invariably, of course, when they read one page they decided to read more. The main problem was just getting to that first page. Once that was done, the rest was not only easy but enjoyable as well.

Get back to the simple pleasure of good reading, one page at a time.

COLLECT GREAT QUESTIONS

NO ONE IN HISTORY HAS MADE PEOPLE *THINK* AS HAS JESUS CHRIST. One of the ways He did so was to ask thought-provoking questions. An example of one of His famous questions is in Matthew 16:15. His disciples were reporting what the crowds were saying about Him. Then Jesus asked the Twelve a question each of us should answer about Him: "But who do you say that I am?"

While preaching a series of sermons on twenty of the questions Jesus asked, my interest in those divinely inspired questions prompted me to begin collecting great questions by others. And I commend the practice because of the help it's been to my spiritual life. I've written the best questions on both sides of a page in my personal organizer. I've divided them into categories: questions for the elderly, young people, church members, and so forth, including general questions appropriate in just about any setting with anyone.

Collecting questions is a lot like collecting stamps, books, or anything else, except it's free. When you hear or read a profound question, add it to your list. Keep the list handy in your organizer, wallet, Bible, or other place where you can easily add to or refer to it. You might also designate a file folder, "Questions," as a simple collecting place for lists of questions or other related material you come across. At this writing, I'm working on my third thick folder and have turned to them countless times. I've also found at least half-a-dozen books of questions that have been helpful.

"But," someone may ask, "how can collecting great questions help simplify my spiritual life?" Good question! For one thing, well-crafted questions put things in focus and help us understand the issues better. As one of my favorite question collectors, Bobb Biehl, said, "Learning to ask is a prerequisite to learning to think clearly."[2]

Framing the issues correctly and thinking about them clearly is at the heart of simplifying the spiritual life.

My spirituality is also simplified by having my list of questions ready when I want to turn a conversation toward the things of God.[3] I often find myself on an airplane with an opportunity to talk with a nonChristian sitting next to me. Sometimes, though, I'm so exhausted that I can't think how to turn the conversation in a more Godward direction. But after a glance at my questions list, the talk soon begins to move toward the things of God.

Keeping great questions handy also simplifies spirituality by providing accessible resources for everything from small-group discussion starters to daily conversations with family and friends. I also appreciate having my cache of thoughtful questions available when I have unexpected opportunities to talk with individuals who have much to teach me about the Bible, spirituality, or anything else. I like the way one of the most influential Christians of the twentieth century, Martyn Lloyd-Jones of London, spoke of the value good questions have for spirituality: "I sometimes think that the whole art of the Christian life is the art of asking questions."[4]

So don't merely collect great questions—ask them. For as New Testament scholar Wayne Detzler wrote, "Ask the right questions and you will become wise."[5]

Walk with the Wise

WE'VE ALL HEARD OF THE THREE "WISE MEN FROM THE EAST" (Matthew 2:1) and the role they played in the story of Jesus' birth. Who are the three wisest people *you* know? Do you know how to gain wisdom like theirs? Wise King Solomon wrote in Proverbs 13:20, "He who walks with wise men will be wise." The wisest men, of course, are in Scripture, for divine inspiration fills their words. And the wisest of them all is the perfect Son of God, Jesus Christ. So if you want "the wisdom that is from above" (James 3:17), go often to the Bible and walk with the wise people who live in its pages.

But what about the wise who have lived *since* the times of the Bible, including the wise people of God alive today? How do we walk with them?

One of the more obvious ways is to read their books and the stories of their lives. Walk with them through the lines they toiled over and let them tell you their best and wisest thoughts. Glean the insights discovered by the biographers who walked with these wise men several hours every day for many months and years.

You can also walk with wise people by hearing them. Go where they will be speaking. Listen to them via radio, the Internet, or recording.

Find a wise person to disciple you. You may know a wise role model, but protest, "He'd never be willing to spend time with me." You'll never know unless you ask. Look for creative ways to offer a skill or service to him in exchange for his wisdom. One of the busiest, most sought-after pastors I know spends two to three hours each week with a young man who offered his services as a personal trainer. As this young man "walks with [the] wise" from one weight machine to another, his soul is trained spiritually and the pastor's body is trained physically.

When you anticipate being with an unusually wise person, prepare a list of questions. One of the most profitable days of my ministry came when I learned that I'd be in a van for hours with several other men, including a couple of well-known, experienced ministers who were driving together to a conference. I made a list of the toughest theological and practical questions in my ministry at the time. I'm sure Solomon would agree that *riding* with wise men can be as profitable as walking with them.

You will become like those with whom you "walk" or spend time. If you spend much of your discretionary hours with foolish or worldly people—including those on TV shows and commercials—you'll grow more foolish and worldly. But if you become one "who walks with wise men [you'll] be wise." Who do you know who's been successful at simplifying spirituality? Walk with that person and you'll simplify yours.

Imitate Spiritual Heroes

MY SPIRITUAL HEROES SURROUND ME WHEN I'M WRITING. THEY SIT on the bookcases on either side of the woodstove. The faces of some of them smile at me from various places on the walls or from nooks at the empty ends of bookshelves. The busts of four look down upon me like Mount Rushmore from a shelf near my computer.

Some would think this spiritually harmful and that it puts my eyes on men instead of Christ. But the Bible tells us to have spiritual heroes. "Remember your leaders, who spoke the word of God to you. Consider the outcome of their way of life and imitate their faith," we're commanded in Hebrews 13:7 (NIV).

All we know of the "leaders" of these Hebrew Christians is found in this text. The words describing their activities are all in the past tense, so these leaders may have died, perhaps even been martyred. They were not to be forgotten, however, and their lives and faith were to be imitated. But the instruction of this passage applies to us as well. Like these Jewish Christians, we should seek godly, truth-speaking heroes too.

The verse tells us first that we should "remember" them, so photos, sculpture, and souvenirs can help. However, this doesn't mean just to remember their features or mannerisms, but to recall things like their love for Christ, their devotion to prayer, and their passion for the gospel and the things of God. One way to do this is to read or listen to biographies of these spiritual heroes.

Second, we should "consider the outcome of their way of life." The Puritan theologian John Owen said the New Testament Greek word translated *consider* means "a repeated, reiterated contemplation of the matter, with its causes and circumstances."[6] Again, the most practical way to think about all these things is to read the accounts of the lives of our spiritual heroes. As we read we should recognize that these are sinful men and women, yet people through whom God worked.

Third, we're told to "imitate their faith." To quote Owen again, "A bare remembrance of them is of little or no use. But to remember them in what they did and taught, so as to follow them . . . , this is a duty of no small advantage to us."[7] One of the advantages of imitating spiritual heroes is the guidance God sometimes gives us through "what they did and taught." They may, for example, show us a pattern for a more simple and effective spiritual life.

Of course, we shouldn't be foolish enough to think that any of our heroes is right about everything. The best of men are men at best. Only one hero is perfect and unchangeable, and He's mentioned in the very next verse: "Jesus Christ is the same yesterday, today, and forever" (Hebrews 13:8). The right heroes will point us to Him.

Having the right heroes also helps protect us from spiritual and theological error. As the following verse warns, "Do not be carried about with various and strange doctrines" (verse 9). All human heroes will lead us into error if we follow them uncritically and without discernment. But to have no heroes for fear of being spiritually polluted is to overreact. The right heroes are right almost all the time. By speaking the Word of God to us, sharing insights we haven't been given, using analogies and illustrations we haven't considered, and formulating truth in ways that make things clear to us, the right heroes will protect us from far more error than they may give us.

Some advocate choosing one spiritual hero, living with him through his biography and books, and making him a spiritual mentor for months or even years. Others prefer a broad range of heroes to an intimate knowledge of only one. Whichever path you choose, find spiritual heroes worthy of remembering, considering, and imitating. And may the Lord speak to you through them to help you simplify and enrich your spiritual life.

REPEAT THE TRUTH

FOR CHRISTIANS WITH A GOOD AND GROWING FAMILIARITY WITH the Scriptures, typically the greater need isn't to learn new truth, but to remember the truth we already know. We are forgetful people, often forgetting even the basic truths of the Bible. And the most helpful thing we could do in the face of many difficulties is simply to remember and repeat the truth.

Jesus frequently emphasized to His twelve disciples the necessity of reminding themselves of the truth in specific situations. On a trip across the Sea of Galilee, the men forgot to bring bread. When they expressed concern, Jesus told them to remember the miracles of provision He had performed earlier: "Do you not yet understand, or remember the five loaves of the five thousand and how many baskets you took up? Nor the seven loaves of the four thousand and how many large baskets you took up?" (Matthew 16:9-10). In other words, Jesus wanted them to remember in this hour of need the truth of how He had provided for them in similar circumstances. "With Jesus and His miraculous power here," they should have remembered, "we don't have to worry about going hungry."

The apostle Paul also taught believers to recall and rest upon the truth. In Acts 20:35, for example, he urged, "Remember the words of the Lord Jesus, that He said, 'It is more blessed to give than to receive.'"

So when you're too discouraged to keep praying that God would change a heart, a child, or a church, learn to repeat the truth to yourself. What *is* the truth for this situation? One important truth is something Jesus taught in Luke 18:1: "Men always ought to pray and not lose heart."

When you're doubtful that the Lord can still love you after what you've done, remember and repeat the truth. For the truth is, "[Nothing] shall be able to separate us from the love of God which is in Christ Jesus our Lord" (Romans 8:39).

When you feel as though the Lord has forgotten you or abandoned you, reinforce this truth in your thinking: "He Himself has said, 'I will never leave you nor forsake you'" (Hebrews 13:5).

When you experience something that tempts you to think, *Nothing good can ever come from this,* remember and rely upon this truth: "And we know that all things work together for good to those who love God, to those who are the called according to His purpose" (Romans 8:28).

Repeating and believing the truth simplifies our spirituality in trying times by helping us to focus on the essentials of our faith when we need them most. Reiterating the truth deepens the impact of the Word of God on our lives by encouraging us to apply God's solutions to real-life problems.

What biblical truth do you especially need to remember right now?

See Everything As an
Illustration of Biblical Truth

MOST PEOPLE DON'T CONSIDER THEMSELVES CREATIVE. BUT ALL OF us, having been made in the image of God *the* Creator, can think creatively. Some do so more easily in music or art, while others think more imaginatively with language, mathematics, or mechanical matters. But everyone has an affinity for creativity in something.

One of the more common forms of creative thought is analogy—gaining insight into one thing by seeing how it is like another. Jesus often taught by analogy in His parables. "The kingdom of heaven is like a man who sowed good seed in his field. . . . The kingdom of heaven . . . is like a mustard seed . . . is like leaven . . . is like treasure hidden in a field . . . is like a merchant seeking beautiful pearls . . . is like a dragnet" (Matthew 13:24,31,33,44,45,47). We always learn more about something we don't know well (in this case, the kingdom of heaven) when it's compared to things we do know well.

Reading the sermons of the famous nineteenth-century preacher Charles Spurgeon makes me believe he saw an illustration of biblical truth in everything. He gave lectures totaling two hundred pages to the students in his pastor's college on the matter of illustration in preaching. Spurgeon devoted three-fourths of his time on the subject to how and where to find illustrations. In summary he said,

> *Find them anywhere.* Anything that occurs around you, if you
> have but brains in your head, will be of service to you; but . . .
> you will need to keep your eyes open. . . . If you do so, you
> will find that, in simply walking through the streets, something or other will suggest a passage of Scripture. . . .

> Try to make comparisons from the things round about you. I
> think it would be well, sometimes, to shut the door . . . and
> say to yourself, "I will not go out of this room until I have
> made at least half-a-dozen illustrations."[8]

Spurgeon's wisdom applies to every Christian, not just those who
preach or teach. So when you see a plane overhead, hear a bird, taste
an orange, feel the cool side of the pillow, smell a rose—ask yourself, "What biblical truth does this illustrate?" Whatever you see or
experience, no matter how small or routine, learn to ask, "How is
this like something in the Bible?"

Most of the creativity in this doesn't flow from mental aptitude,
but from a simple, intentional looking. The more you intentionally
look for illustrations of biblical truth, the more insight you'll have
into Scripture. And the more you'll find yourself setting "your mind
on things above, not on things on the earth" (Colossians 3:2).

THINK MUCH ABOUT HEAVEN

THE MOST HEAVENLY-MINDED MAN WHO EVER LIVED—JESUS AND other biblical characters excepted—may have been Richard Baxter. He was a remarkable Puritan pastor and writer who lived for seventy-six years (1615–1691), despite suffering with one physical malady or another almost constantly. During the winter of 1646, ill health forced him to spend several lonely months in a house far from his home and family. His condition was so grave that he was "sentenced to death by the physicians."[9]

With his life ebbing away, Baxter began thinking much about Heaven. As he put it, "I began to contemplate more seriously on the everlasting rest which I apprehended myself to be just on the borders of." As he was able, and so that "[his] thoughts might not too much scatter in [his] meditation,"[10] he wrote out his meditations that he might review and be comforted by them. These were the beginning of perhaps the most important of his 140 books, *The Saints' Everlasting Rest*, published four years later. He found his extended times of meditation on Heaven so helpful that, after his recovery, he continued them for the remaining five decades of his life. For half-an-hour each day, usually while walking before dinner, Baxter disciplined his mind to focus on the world to come. As a result of becoming so heavenly-minded, he became one of the most earthly-good men of his or any other time. Many of his books, as well as the example of his pastoral method (recorded in *The Reformed Pastor*), continue their influence centuries after his death.

Fixing your thoughts on Heaven can be a powerful practice, because there is nothing on earth to compare with the beauty, splendor, and joy of that place. To think rightly about Heaven is much more than anticipating the rest and reunions there. That's not distinctively Christian thinking; even atheists want those things. In addition to these wonderful blessings, Christians yearn to gaze on the irresistible face of Jesus and to bask in the undiminished glory of Him whose countenance is "like the sun shining in its strength" (Revelation 1:16). We groan as we longingly imagine the glorious freedom of a mind and body without sin, "eagerly waiting for the adoption, the redemption of our body" (Romans 8:23).

So "set your mind on things above, not on things on the earth" (Colossians 3:2). Let your Scripture-guided imagination wonder what living in that perfect world will be like. Doing so will simplify your spiritual life by helping you to see your spirituality (and everything else) more from the perspective of eternity. It will clarify your priorities. It will remind you of a coming glory that's worth any suffering here, knowing that "our light affliction, which is but for a moment, is working for us a far more exceeding and eternal weight of glory" (2 Corinthians 4:17).

Thinking much about Heaven—"heavenly meditation" as Richard Baxter called it—will transform us, just as it transformed him. Baxter's example of thirty minutes daily may be unrealistic for most, but thinking about the greatest, most magnificent, and most alluring of all objects is worth all the time we can devote to it.

SIMPLIFYING
AND
YOUR
HEART

SANCTIFY YOUR SUFFERINGS AS SPIRITUALITY

MY PREACHER-HERO OF THE TWENTIETH CENTURY, MARTYN LLOYD-Jones, made a perceptive observation about John Bunyan's timeless allegory of the Christian life, *Pilgrim's Progress:* "The great truth in Bunyan's *Pilgrim's Progress* is not that Christian endured great hardships on his way to the eternal city, but that Christian thought it to be worth his while to endure those hardships."[1]

Those familiar with Bunyan's classic will know that most of Christian's hardships—and certainly his most difficult ones—were not those common to everyone. His most agonizing troubles were those he suffered internally and externally precisely because he was following Christ. But he found them all, even the life-threatening ones, "worth his while" in light of what he anticipated at the end of his journey.

As you're reading this, tens of thousands of the Lord's pilgrims around the world are threatened with execution, torture, slavery, starvation, homelessness, poverty, imprisonment, and other persecutions designed to destroy their faith in Jesus Christ. And yet, despite many of the same kinds of evil cruelty hurled at Jesus Himself, they find it "worth [their] while to endure those hardships" because of what they have and hope for in Christ. With far more than words, they prove they believe that "our light affliction, which is but for a moment, is working for us a far more exceeding and eternal weight of glory" (2 Corinthians 4:17).

Even if we do not pay the ultimate price of dying for our devotion to the One who died for us, everyone who wants to live for Christ will suffer for it. For "all who desire to live godly in Christ Jesus will suffer persecution" (2 Timothy 3:12). But when we do suffer for being a Christian, or even when we experience the same hardships that unbelievers do, we should sanctify our sufferings as part of our spirituality.

For example, when persecuted for our faith, our endurance testifies to the worthiness of Christ. Unrelenting faithfulness in the absence of all earthly explanation says to the watching world, "It is worth enduring all this pain and heartache to know Christ and to anticipate the glory of being with Him forever." And when we grieve and groan under the hardships that grind Christians and nonChristians alike, we sanctify our sufferings when we draw closer to Christ because of them.

Thinking this way helps to simplify the spiritual life because it simplifies our understanding of the nature of spirituality. Instead of mentally cloistering our spirituality to the strictly religious areas of life (such as devotional habits or church), this approach enables us to realize that in some sense everything is spirituality, even our sufferings. Those who suffer best realize that even the worst and most painful parts of life relate directly to the soul and to our walk with God.

In all suffering, may God give us the grace to live with faith, remembering what the apostle Paul proclaimed in Romans 8:18: "For I consider that the sufferings of this present time are not worthy to be compared with the glory which shall be revealed in us."

Happy is he for whom the hope of glory in "the eternal city" makes any suffering "worth his while."

KILL YOUR SINS

IN APRIL 1983, ROBERT VIERLING OF WINCHESTER, MISSOURI, WAS found on his bed, crushed to death by his sixteen-foot, one-hundred-pound, pet Burmese python. Vierling's wife said he had complete trust in the snake and often played with it on the bed. Each of us lives with many unseen snakes, all more deadly than a Burmese python. These snakes, which are constantly with us, are called "sins" in the Bible. The process of killing them is called mortification.

The doctrine of mortification is seldom heard today, partly because the word *mortify* is a King James term that's rendered "put to death" in modern translations. But mortification is absolutely critical, for the Bible says that even though killing the snakes of sin in our lives won't get us to Heaven — only the life and death of Jesus Christ can do that — unless we bring deadly violence against them all our lives, we've never experienced the saving work of Christ.

God's Word teaches this in Romans 8:12-13: "Therefore, brethren, we are debtors — not to the flesh, to live according to the flesh. For if you live according to the flesh you will die; but if by the Spirit you put to death the deeds of the body, you will live." In other words, if we complacently live by the deeds and desires God calls sinful, we will suffer certain spiritual death and its eternal consequences. But if, by the Holy Spirit, we constantly struggle to kill these sinful deeds and desires, we show that we really possess and will forever enjoy eternal life through Jesus Christ.

Mortification of sin is extremely important, but why mention it in a book on simplifying our spirituality? It's here because mortification does simplify the spiritual life by telling us clearly what we must do with the single most complicating factor in our lives — sin — and why. The Bible says we must kill our sins, not tolerate or excuse them in the name of grace, or they will kill us.

In our ongoing war with our sins, we should also remember other Bible truths that complement our understanding and practice of mortification. These include the eternal forgiveness of all the sins of all believers through the cross of Jesus, the grace of God preserving His people to the end, and the truth that in this life we'll never experience the permanent removal of all sin or the desire to sin. Consistent with them all is this teaching in Romans 8:12-13 that, regardless of our professed beliefs, one evidence that Christ has truly saved us is a lethal, lifelong fight against every sin we commit.

In January 2001, the Reuters news network reported the story of South African Lucas Sibanda, who was attacked by a python. Trapped in the snake's constricting coil, Sibanda bit the reptile below the head and kicked and punched until it released its grip. Then he killed the python with a stick.

Pythons of sin will attack and fight against us all our lives. Unless by the Holy Spirit we fight back like Lucas Sibanda, we show that there is no spiritual life in us.

Get deadly serious with your sins.

Sing Your Spirituality

Leonard Roper was my maternal grandfather, and we grand-kids called him Pappaw. After marrying my grandmother in 1919, he settled into the routines of farming the red clay hills of northeast Mississippi. At daylight each morning he harnessed the mules and headed them to the fields. At noon he rested against a tree, taking his lunch from one of the buckets he'd brought, and drinking water from another. This was his life Monday through Saturday, throughout the Roaring Twenties, throughout the Great Depression, throughout World War II, year after year.

My mother's earliest memory of him is not a scene, but a sound. Before she could see him following the team through the hedgerow each evening, she could hear him singing. Plodding back in overalls and field hat, Pappaw sang his way home in the dusk.

His was a simple life and a simple faith. And while our lives are very different from his, this melodic aspect of his spirituality may help simplify ours.

I'm sure you sing just about every day already—while dressing, driving, working, cleaning, and at odd moments throughout the day—with or without music in the background. But what do you sing? I want to encourage you to extend your spirituality even into these times by more deliberately "singing and making melody in your heart to the *Lord*" (Ephesians 5:19, emphasis addded). In other words, let's be more intentional about "singing . . . to the Lord" throughout the week, and not just on Sunday.

So when you catch yourself purposelessly singing something of little value, sing your spirituality instead. Shift gears in your soul from oldies and jingles and worldly songs to "psalms and hymns and spiritual songs" (Colossians 3:16). Find the songs you do want to keep in your mind, and play them in your car/home sound system. For a more structured approach, use a hymnal in your personal and family worship. Sing the same song to the Lord every day for three or four weeks in personal and/or family worship, and you'll probably hear yourself singing it at other times too.

A songless Christian is a contradiction in terms, for the Bible describes God's people as those who say, "He has put a new song in my mouth—praise to our God" (Psalm 40:3). If He has put that new song in your mouth, sing it every day.

CLARIFY YOUR AMBITION

"HE'S VERY AMBITIOUS."

Is that a compliment or a criticism?

Do you want to be known as ambitious?

Would you prefer to be known as someone who has no ambition?

We know it's not like Christ to climb over people, to politick for influence, or to be driven blindly for wealth, position, or fame. But it's also unChristian to be slothful, dispassionate about the quality of your work, or without motivation.

Hmmm. Ambitious: to be or not to be?

Your answer to this question will influence the contours of your spirituality, so one way to simplify your spirituality is to clarify your ambition. A biblical starting place is to recognize that two very different kinds of ambition are described in the New Testament.

The first is often presented as "selfish ambition" or "self-seeking." This kind of ambition strains for personal gain at almost any cost. It's the sort of ambition that characterizes the ungodly (see Galatians 5:20) and those under the wrath of God (see Romans 2:8). Self-seeking ambition has a partner: "bitter envy." Together they often push a person to "boast and lie" (James 3:14) in order to get ahead or to hold others back. And in any heart, home, or workplace "where envy and self-seeking exist, confusion and every evil thing are there" (James 3:16). Is there a more succinct description of a complicated life than one where "confusion and every evil thing" abound?

But there's another kind of ambition described in the New Testament. We're ambitious in a holy sense when we eagerly aspire for something that is right and good in God's sight. Such ambition may be for things great or small, as long as the goal, method, and motivation are God-centered.

The apostle Paul exuded this good ambition when he determined to preach where no one had heard of Jesus: "It has always been my ambition to preach the gospel where Christ was not known" (Romans 15:20, NIV). Like Paul, and in obedience to the Lord's Great Commission (see Matthew 28:19-20), part of our own holy ambition should relate to the spread of the good news of Jesus Christ.

The Lord reveals another aspect of the right kind of ambition in the command of 1 Thessalonians 4:11: "make it your ambition to lead a quiet life" (NASB). That doesn't mean we shouldn't, in the famous words of pioneer missionary William Carey, "attempt great things for God." Instead it speaks to the object of our ambition. Ourselves, or God? The unrelenting drive of selfish ambition never leads to a quiet life. Only when our ambition is to have no *selfish* ambition can we hope for a quieter life.

God may choose to give us a not-so-quiet life. But there's a world of difference between a busy life where everything is ordered around the Lord and one filled with "confusion and every evil thing."

Regardless of the size, scope, or pace of our pursuits, we should always "have as our ambition . . . to be pleasing to Him" (2 Corinthians 5:9, NASB). Whenever this ambition falls second to selfish ambition, the spiritual life will decline. The demands of the higher affection will steal time from the spiritual disciplines. And eventually this leads to a more complicated and frustrating life.

For what—or rather for *whom*—are you living? Clarify your ambition and you'll significantly simplify your spiritual life.

Minimize Electronic Spirituality, Part 1

I ALMOST USED THE WORD "DELETE" INSTEAD OF "MINIMIZE" IN THE title of this chapter. However, electronic spirituality — that is, using resources like the computer and the Internet for the sake of the soul — can be practical at times. When the spiritual need of the moment is information, computer-driven resources will usually provide more information and present it faster than any alternative. For example, if you need a Bible and don't have one with you, being able to read the electronic text from a screen is a great blessing. Other than extreme circumstances like this, however, pull the plug on electronic spirituality.

In general, Christians engage in electronic spirituality in two broad ways — individually and interpersonally. Here I am addressing the former, that is, when individual believers pursue their devotional practices of Bible intake and prayer by means of a computer or the Internet. Note that I am distinguishing between devotional experiences and study. While book-based study has its advantages over electronic processes, admittedly there are times when the accessibility and speed of electronic tools argues for their use in Bible study and other research.

It's not surprising for people accustomed to doing almost everything else in front of a computer to practice their personal spiritual disciplines there too. I know, for instance, of believers who are committed to communing with the Lord in private each day, but do so after getting their daily Scripture passages and other devotional readings emailed to them or after the text pops up automatically on the computer screen morning by morning like electronic manna.

Remember, however, that a daily time of worship before the Lord is the seeking of a Person, not just information. In these moments the Lord bids us, as in Psalm 27:8, "Seek My face," not mere facts. We come to these times to relate to our God, not to a machine. Can't we relate to God through words on a screen as well as through words on a printed page? Yes, we *can,* for the power is in God's Word, not in the format by which it is read. But I question whether it is either easier or simpler to relate to God through an electronic device than otherwise. Dealing with a computer is proverbial for an impersonal experience. "I hate it when a computer answers the phone instead of a real person," we complain. Why, then, especially since we have other means available, would we want to use such an impersonal means to relate to the most important Person in our lives?

When your individual spirituality becomes more dependent on technology, your devotional experience can be derailed by hardware crashes, software glitches, connectivity problems, power failures, and other technical contingencies. And besides the ordinary distractions when trying to meditate on the text of Scripture or focus on the Lord, doing this in front of a screen also subjects you to the distractions of incoming email and other sounds or messages produced by your computer.

Quicker computer speeds and faster Internet connections do not upgrade intimacy with Jesus. Despite its allurements or convenience, electronic spirituality does nothing to improve individual spirituality that cannot be gained by simpler means. Minimize electronic spirituality and simplify your spiritual life.

Build the Wealth of Simplicity with Contentment

Wealth comes in many forms. In today's world, one form of wealth is simplicity. The more freedom one has from the frustrations of an increasingly complex world, the wealthier he is. And one of the ways of simplifying the spiritual life is to learn contentment.

The apostle Paul once warned his younger colleague, Timothy, about devious men who enter the ministry and deceive people through false piety in hopes of making money. He spoke of them as those "who suppose that godliness is a means of gain" (1 Timothy 6:5). Then Paul said, "Now godliness with contentment is great gain" (verse 6). In other words, *true* godliness—the kind "with contentment" instead of greed—really "is great gain." How so?

The Christian who learns contentment experiences the "great gain" of freedom from a complex web of evils that have eternally ruined the souls of many. As verse 9 explains, contentment frees you from the "temptation and a snare, and . . . many foolish and harmful lusts which drown men in destruction and perdition." Contentment greatly minimizes the possibility that greed will prove you to be a false, self-deceived Christian, as it has "some [who] have strayed from the faith in their greediness, and pierced themselves through with many sorrows" (verse 10).

*Dis*contentment, whether about income or anything else, complicates life. It demands the pursuit of more money or things than you have now. Since more cannot satisfy, the discontentment grows and pushes you harder and faster. And as the pace of life increases, so does its complexity.

But the Bible exhorts us, "Be content with such things as you have" (Hebrews 13:5). How can the Lord expect that of us? It's because in the same verse, "He Himself has said, 'I will never leave you nor forsake you.'" Regardless of what we do *not* have, knowing that we'll never lose the riches of the presence of the Lord Himself should content us "with such things as [we] have." And this kind of Christ-centered contentment liberates us from the complicating pursuit of more and builds the wealth of simplicity. Enjoy the wealth.

LEARN TO BE CONTENT

CONTENTMENT IS A GREAT SIMPLIFIER. IT HELPS FOCUS BODY AND soul on the proper priorities. It calms the restless desire for more. It satisfies the heart with the present provision of God. It deflates pride, drains the drive of selfish ambition, and relaxes the grip of anxiety. Contentment decreases our dependence upon things and circumstances, and increases a restful dependence upon Christ.

The apostle Paul spoke of developing contentment in his own experience when he said, "I have learned in whatever state I am, to be content: I know how to be abased, and I know how to abound. Everywhere and in all things I have learned both to be full and to be hungry, both to abound and to suffer need. I can do all things through Christ who strengthens me" (Philippians 4:11-13).

Notice that Paul speaks of contentment as something to be *learned*. One way that we, like Paul, can learn contentment is to recognize the true value of things. To do this, we can learn when we are "full" and we "abound" in material things why the abundance of them cannot content us. Unlike our souls, touchable things will not last. What's more, God never designed tangible and temporal things to satisfy the intangible and eternal part of us. Material things cannot make us right with God, nor provide any benefit extending into our eternity. How can we find contentment in things so temporary and inconsequential?

At the opposite extreme, recognizing the true value of things also teaches contentment when, like Paul, we are "hungry" and "suffer need." This is no superficial, untested contentment Paul experienced. His suffering and needs were real and prolonged, yet he was genuinely content. He could even be content when forced to go hungry. And don't confuse such contentment with apathy or laziness, for elsewhere the apostle reminds his readers how he worked whenever possible to meet his own physical needs (see 1 Thessalonians 2:9; 2 Thessalonians 3:7-8). What Paul models and advocates is a circumstance-conquering contentment that does not depend on how much there is to eat, spend, wear, count, collect, or touch.

When a person can be content "everywhere and in all things," whether full or hungry, abounding or suffering need, he knows a source of contentment beyond anything the world can provide or understand. True contentment in all places and circumstances is found only, as Paul put it, "through Christ who strengthens me." Only Jesus could have given Paul the contentment to sing at midnight in a filthy, rat-infested prison, with his feet in stocks and his back mercilessly and illegally bloodied (see Acts 16:22-25). Christ, and Christ alone, can strengthen our souls to be content in any and all situations. But this contentment doesn't come unawares. We must be willing to learn it, and to learn it through Christ.

Where do you think He wants to begin your education in contentment?

Learn to Be Content with Christ

No one will satisfyingly simplify his spiritual life without developing contentment. Contentment is a Christian virtue that requires development, for it does not emerge fully formed at conversion. Rather, as the apostle Paul's example reminds us, contentment is learned. "I have learned," he writes in Philippians 4:11, "in whatever state I am, to be content." And the source of his contentment "everywhere and in all things" (verse 12) was this: "I can do all things through Christ who strengthens me" (verse 13).

One of the ways Paul teaches us to learn contentment is to *learn the true value of things.* As we do, we'll learn that contentment cannot be based on them. That's how Paul learned to be content whether he was "full" and "abound[ing]" in material possessions, or whether he was "hungry" and "suffer[ing] need" (verse 12).

But the main way Paul learned contentment was by *learning the value of Christ.* According to verse 13, what Paul found in Christ strengthened his soul to be content regardless of his circumstances. And God inspired and preserved Paul's words so that we too might experience the same contenting depth of riches in Christ.

We can be content in Christ, regardless of our circumstances, because in Him we have everything we need, for now and forever (see Colossians 2:10). How can we not be content if we realize that as believers in Christ we are "joint heirs with Christ" (Romans 8:17), and will inherit everything from the Father that Christ inherits? How can we remain discontented when we realize the implications of verses like Romans 8:32: "He who did not spare His own Son, but delivered Him up for us all, how shall He not with Him also freely give us all things?" God the Father has already given us the greatest and most fulfilling gift possible—God the Son. And in addition to

Him, our Father will "freely give us all things" necessary in this life as well. Knowing, therefore, the infinite value of Christ, we can be content.

The essence of contentment is being satisfied with the incomparable and limitless treasures found in Jesus Christ. Contentment is your soul saying, "I have Jesus, and Jesus is enough."

SIMPLIFYING
AND
YOUR
TIME

Discipline Yourself

Tomorrow morning, I don't have to decide if I'm going to read God's Word and spend time in prayer to Him. Meeting with the Lord is a discipline long-rooted in my morning routines, and my commitment to it simplifies my spirituality. It's one less decision I have to make, one more spiritual priority well woven into the fabric of my daily life.

The apostle Paul instructs us, "Discipline yourself for the purpose of godliness" (1 Timothy 4:7, NASB). The practical ways of fleshing out obedience to this command are called the Christian spiritual disciplines, the God-given means by which we are to bring ourselves before the Lord. And as we enjoy a growing relationship with Him through them, He changes us "for the purpose of godliness," that is, He makes us more like Jesus. And so, as we practice these disciplines, our lives conform more to biblical—and simpler—rhythms and patterns.

In one way, when you enjoy a simpler spiritual life than you have now, it will still be—and *should* be—busy. If you obediently pursue both the Great Commandment and the Great Commission of Jesus (see Mark 12:28-31; Matthew 28:18-20), as well as "discipline yourself for the purpose of godliness," you won't grow idle. But even though the personal and congregational spiritual disciplines lead to a full life, they can also simplify it.

For example, the Christian spiritual disciplines help us focus on the right things, including the most important of all: knowing and glorifying God. Conversely, practicing the disciplines also helps prevent some bad habits, such as spending time in nonproductive, unwise, or even sinful ways. Personally, I have the clearest vision, both of what I should bring into and carve from my life, while engaged in spiritual disciplines like meditating on Scripture, praying through Scripture, or worshiping the Lord with His people.

The disciplines simplify our spiritual lives further by simplifying our communion with God. He hasn't left us to find our own ways to Him. We don't have to wonder how to meet with the Lord and experience Him. God Himself established paths—such as Bible intake, prayer, worship, service, evangelism, fasting, silence and solitude, journaling, and fellowship—which make our spiritual walk with Him simpler and more satisfying.

No one coasts into Christlikeness. Any progress in godliness requires Spirit-filled effort and purpose. But the Christian spiritual disciplines, rightly practiced, can bring some simplicity and order to the process of becoming more like Jesus. Where do you need to "discipline yourself for the purpose of godliness"?

DISCIPLINE YOURSELF . . . WITHOUT LEGALISM

MY WIFE, CAFFY, AND I HAVE A LONGTIME FRIEND WHO ASKED ME about the book I was writing. When I told her the title was *Simplify Your Spiritual Life,* she responded abruptly with, "No rules."

"What do you mean?"

"There should be no rules for the spiritual life. I try to read in four different places in my Bible every day, but some days I read in only two or three. I don't want a rule that says I *have* to read four."

But the Bible itself gives us *some* rules about our spirituality. One of them, for example, is in 1 Timothy 4:7: "Discipline yourself for the purpose of godliness" (NASB). In obedience to this command, every Christian should pursue intimacy with Christ and the imitation of Christ through the practice of the personal and congregational spiritual disciplines found in Scripture. What we should oppose is measuring this pursuit by rules that aren't in the Bible.

So, while the Scripture commands us to engage in the spiritual disciplines, we don't want to pursue them legalistically. Legalism is the improper emphasis on works in our relationship to God. It focuses on the manifestations of spirituality that can be measured by number, frequency, duration, amount, and so forth. No one has the authority to force upon themselves or anyone else external measurements of spirituality that have no scriptural basis. Thus, it would be legalistic to tell our friend that she must read four places in the Bible every day, or even that she *must* read her Bible on a daily basis at all.

The opposite of legalism is license, that is, living as though freedom in Christ means there are *no* measurable standards of spirituality. License leads a person to presume he can be faithful to the Lord's word in 1 Timothy 4:7, even if he *never* reads the Bible again.

The spiritually disciplined Christian life should be lived

between these two errors. On the one hand, because of the grace of God experienced through Christ, believers are free from keeping manmade rules as a way of keeping the love of God. "Stand fast therefore," says Galatians 5:1, "in the liberty by which Christ has made us free, and do not be entangled again with a yoke of bondage."

On the other hand, because of the same heart-changing grace of God at work in us "both to will and to do for His good pleasure" (Philippians 2:13), we sincerely *want* to discipline ourselves to pursue godliness. And the fact of the matter is that these biblical disciplines (such as Bible intake, prayer, worship, fellowship, stewardship, and fasting) can all be measured in one way or another. What matters is *why* we measure them. If it's to reassure ourselves of our soul's condition based on our external performance, then we're acting like Pharisees.

But if we measure particular aspects of our disciplines in order to simplify our spiritual lives or to hold ourselves accountable to certain goals, then there may be real benefits. So a person might try to read a given number of chapters in the Bible daily in order to avoid deciding every single day how much to read, and/or to keep pace for reading through the Bible in a year.

Not even the most rigorous practice of the spiritual disciplines is legalistic when the motives of our spirituality are what they should be, namely, to do all to the glory of God and to pursue Christlikeness.

Practice Spiritual Multi-Tasking

Multi-tasking sounds like something we want to avoid when simplifying our spiritual lives. And while that's probably true in general, there are exceptions to the rule.

Multi-tasking originated as a technological term to speak of a computer performing more than one function at a time, but it makes me think of plate spinners who performed in variety shows in the days of black-and-white TV. A plate spinner would balance a dinner plate on top of a tall, pencil-thin wooden rod, then strike the plate's edge to make it spin. Then he would quickly start a second one spinning on another rod, then a third, on up to about ten or twelve. By the time he'd started the last one, the first plates would begin to wobble, so he'd run to the beginning of the line and quickly give each a new spin.

Sometimes people think that by advocating the number of spiritual disciplines I mention in this book and in places like *Spiritual Disciplines for the Christian Life* I'm encouraging them to be spiritual plate spinners. They picture themselves trying to keep an overwhelming number of disciplines balanced, spending more time concerned about the mere maintenance of them than the fruit of them.

Just because we can isolate a discipline (like prayer, Bible intake, worship, or fasting) and examine it doesn't necessarily mean that it is *practiced* in isolation from other disciplines. In fact, it's not unusual to perform five or six disciplines during the same devotional period, most of them simultaneously.

For example, simply by having a "quiet time," you are practicing one form of the discipline of silence and solitude. And during that time you will likely engage in worship, Bible intake, and prayer.

That's three more disciplines. Many will also write their insights from Scripture, their meditations, or other entries into a journal during this time. And if you happen to be fasting, that's half-a-dozen individual disciplines being performed during the same devotional period. You're doing more than you realize.

So while we can distinguish various spiritual disciplines, we do not always have to separate them. Spiritual multi-tasking is not about spinning many spiritual plates; it's about many ways of filling your one spiritual plate with delicious, satisfying, divine nourishment for your soul.

REMIND YOURSELF

Do you ever resolve to make some changes in your spiritual life, and then fail to make them? More importantly, do you ever make commitments to God and then fail to keep them? Yes, I know. Me too.

Sometimes, though, my problem is not an intentional disobedience; rather, it is forgetfulness. There are changes I want to make that I often fail to make, not because I wasn't sincere, but because I was too busy to change *without frequent reminders* of the commitment I made.

There have been times, for instance, when I intended to pray several times daily for a particular person or situation. But without some means of reminding myself of my new resolve, my daily routines bred a forgetfulness of my good intention.

One way I've found to simplify in this matter is to insert visible reminders into some part of my daily routines, typically my devotional routines. For instance, one method I've used for years is to draw a small rectangular box of six squares (two rows of three) at the beginning of the first line of my journal entry for the day. Each box reminds me of a goal for my spiritual life for that day, six practices that I tend to forget. This is not legalism, for my spiritual standing is based on Christ's righteousness, not upon my inconsistent, self-imposed standards. Rather, these are things I want (not have) to do, and I know myself well enough to realize that without some sort of reminder I likely will forget them.

Here's another technique I sometimes use. During the course of a day, I will try to write fifteen times the commitment I've made or the action I want to take. This can be done on a note card, on a sheet of paper, on a page in a daily calendar, on a computer document, on a sticky note, or wherever else works. I find this method effective because it keeps my commitment before me throughout the day, even on the busiest of days. And during the few moments it takes to write it out each time, I'm prompted to pray for the Lord's grace and power to do what I believe He would have me to do.

You could also jog your memory by means of an automatic reminder on the computer or other electronic device you use, regularly reviewing a list of self-examination questions, or anything else that helps you to remember commitments and translate them into actions.

Proverbs 13:4 observes, "The soul of a lazy man desires, and has nothing; but the soul of the diligent shall be made rich." Note that the soul of both the sluggard and the diligent desires something, but only the soul of the diligent is enriched. That's because he took action to fulfill his desires and the sluggard didn't. Finding some frequent means to remind yourself of your spiritual desires is one way of turning them into reality.

The apostle Paul didn't mind reiterating things that his readers especially needed to remember. "For me to write the same things to you is not tedious, but for you it is safe" (Philippians 3:1). Neither did the apostle Peter hesitate to remind his readers of the truths they were prone to forget: "For this reason I will not be negligent to remind you always of these things, though you know and are established in the present truth" (2 Peter 1:12).

What truths, commitments, or resolves—perhaps even about simplifying your spiritual life—do you need help remembering? Find some simple, regular, visible means to remind yourself.

REMOVE ONE THING, ORGANIZE ONE THING

SIMPLIFYING YOUR SPIRITUAL LIFE SHOULD HAVE AN IMPACT ON EVERY other part of life. However, it's also true that if other parts of your life are exasperatingly complex, they can damage your spirituality. So it's worth looking at ways to simplify in other areas because of the influence that may have on you spiritually.

For instance, there's a point where clutter and disorganization affect my spirituality. A workable strategy I often use is to remove one thing from my home or office each day and to organize one thing each day. To remind myself to do this, I write, "Remove one thing" and "Organize one thing," as separate items on my to-do list for a number of days.

Following this plan doesn't take much time (usually), it's not overwhelming, and it's not impractical, all because I'm dealing with such small numbers of things. And because it's so measurable, I can immediately see that I'm making real progress. This plan makes clutter removal and getting organized much more realistic. It also helps reduce my dependence on things.

So one day I might pull a book from my shelves and put it with those I'll sell at a used bookstore, and organize part of my desktop. Another day I might remove an item of clothing from the closet for donation to a thrift store, then rearrange one shelf in the closet. A third day I might put an unused radio in a box of items to be sold at a garage sale, and find places for things I've been piling on the floor.

Anyone well acquainted with me knows that I have a long way to go with removing and organizing clutter—in many areas of my life. In fact, this struggle is one of the reasons I felt the need to research and write this book. If you can identify with my struggle, maybe the "Remove one thing, organize one thing" principle will work for you as it has for me.

File It, for the Sake of Your Soul

YOU PROBABLY KEEP FILES FOR MANY THINGS: TAXES, PRODUCT warranties, coupons, manuals, receipts, bank statements, and so forth. Why not keep files for the sake of your soul?

Although much of what I file has to do with being a preacher and a writer, anyone can adapt the idea to make it workable and edifying for his own situation.

I keep two sets of files: biblical and topical. I have sixty-six in the first set, one for each book of the Bible. Into these go my quiet-time meditations on specific texts, study notes, as well as any Scripture-related material from others that will be helpful to me later.

The topical files include headings like Abortion, Baptism, Christ, Church, Cross, Discipleship, Evangelism, Fellowship, and whatever else I want. Only as the need arises do I add new files. Of course, if you're just beginning to collect and organize such information, you'll add files more frequently.

Whenever I read a useful article in a newspaper or magazine, I'll clip it and place it in the appropriate file. Often I receive an email or find something on the Internet I'll want to print and keep for future reference. When I buy a new book, I may photocopy the table of contents and place it in one or more files. Then when I open the file(s), I'm reminded that I also have a book on that subject. On many occasions, if it had not been for my file, I would not have remembered I had a book with a very profitable section on my topic, because the book was primarily about another or several other subjects.

And that's the point. With this simple method, when I want something I've saved, I can easily find it. When I need help on a particular passage or with a specific subject, I can go to the appropriate file and find a number of resources waiting for me. After doing this for several decades, if I suddenly had to decide between keeping my files or the thousands of books in my library, I'd choose my files in a heartbeat. Most of my books could be replaced. It would be impossible to restore my files.

Which is more important, keeping your lawnmower manual or materials that can benefit your eternal soul? Why not do both? The uncomplicated discipline of keeping a basic filing system is one way to "discipline yourself for the purpose of godliness" (1 Timothy 4:7, NASB).

RECOGNIZE THE SPIRITUALITY OF WORK

BILL OFTEN WONDERS WHETHER HE IS A SECOND-CLASS CHRISTIAN because of the less-than-Christian atmosphere he works in every day. His occupation is good and necessary for society, but it's also a line of work known for its liars, cheats, and thieves. Vulgar and blasphemous language typically fills the air of Bill's workplace.

For other believers, the problem at work is not a godless environment; it's the gnawing lack of meaning to their labor. They trudge through tedious days on jobs that often seem intolerably unimportant.

Can followers of Jesus work in these conditions and still maintain a close relationship with Him? Or is the Lord somewhat disappointed in them because of where they work and what they do?

God ordained work. *Before* sin entered the world, "the LORD God took the man [Adam] and put him in the garden of Eden to tend and keep it" (Genesis 2:15). All kinds of work—paid and unpaid—are necessary in the world for us to "subdue it" according to God's will (Genesis 1:28). People must grow food, care for children, make clothes, tend the sick, build buildings and roads, transport goods, govern cities, and so forth. Obviously, therefore, God intends for most people to devote themselves to what's often called "secular" employment. Only a small percentage should be vocational pastors, church-planting missionaries, and the like (even though more are needed). Otherwise, who'd work the fields, deliver the mail, build ships and cars, develop water systems, and make medicines?

Because God has ordained it, all work has a spiritual dimension. The Bible repeatedly commends useful, honest labor (see Ephesians 4:28; 1 Thessalonians 4:11; 2 Thessalonians 3:10), which shows

God's intense interest in it. When we recognize His presence in the workplace, we acknowledge His sovereignty over all of life.

Even if your daily responsibilities seem dull and unimportant, or cause you to associate with and support worldly, God-hating people, remember that "the LORD takes pleasure in His people" (Psalm 149:4). And He takes pleasure in us not just at church, but at work too. He's as attentive to you in your work routines as He was to Joseph in his service as Potiphar's slave, to Jesus in the carpentry shop, and to the apostle Paul when he was making tents.

Work is not a hindrance to spirituality; it is a part of it. Secular work is not a condition unbecoming to a Christian. Secular work is not inconsistent with or a contradiction to or a limitation to Christian spirituality. Even slaves were instructed by Paul not to fear that their awful condition in any way diminished their spiritual standing with God (see 1 Corinthians 7:22). Our spirituality depends upon who we are in Christ, not upon circumstances of our workplace. God's presence and favor are not limited by coworkers or job descriptions.

Enlarge your vision of your spiritual life to include your daily work. "And whatever you do, do it heartily, as to the Lord and not to men, knowing that from the Lord you will receive the reward of the inheritance; for you serve the Lord Christ" (Colossians 3:23-24). Present your work to God. You are working for Him.

Do What You Can

I ADMIRE JEAN FLEMING. SHE'S BEEN BOTH A HOME AND OVERSEAS missionary. She boldly and winsomely shares her faith, makes a priority of discipling other Christian women, and leads Bible studies. She actively supports her husband's full-time ministry, frequently opens her home for Christian hospitality, and serves in her local church. In her home and halfway across the country she has cared for both physically and mentally impaired relatives for long periods. The Flemings have raised three children and now enjoy their role as grandparents. Through it all Jean has written several books and articles.

She was converted in her late teens. Discipled well from the start, Jean thrived on a spiritual diet strong on disciplines like the reading, studying, and meditating on God's Word, prayer, fellowship, service, evangelism, worship, silence and solitude, journal keeping, and Scripture memory. She felt herself making spiritual progress almost daily. All this continued after she married her equally dedicated husband, Roger.

Then she had three children in diapers. Caring for their most basic needs eliminated almost every moment of the time she used to devote to caring for her soul. Her longings for the things of God reached as high as ever, but her time and energy had new and severe limits.

On at least three occasions I've eavesdropped as Jean addressed young moms in similar situations. In effect, she's told them, "At this time in your life, you can't do what you're used to doing. You don't have time for all your heart desires to experience in your spiritual life. Nevertheless, do what you can do, even though it's precious little. Just don't deceive yourself by thinking that you can put off a devotional life until you have more time. Because when the years roll

around and you finally do have more time, your spiritual habits will
be so ingrained that you won't give more attention to your devotional life at all."

Then I heard Jean tell her own story. She would keep Bibles
open in several rooms—in the kitchen, nursery, bathroom—and
look at them when she could. While warming a bottle or changing
a diaper, she'd glance over and perhaps read only one verse. But this
discipline helped her keep the Word in her heart and the presence of
God in her awareness. And as the children's needs grew less demand-
ing, her disciplines were already in place to receive any additional
time she could give them. Even though Jean felt almost spiritually
dormant during those years in comparison to her early growth as a
Christian, she kept alive the spiritual disciplines through which her
soul would blossom in years to come.

Like Jean with three in diapers, you may be in a situation that
curtails many of your spiritual activities. You may be looking at
many months or even years of such limitations. Do what you can.
God does not love us more when we do more, nor less when we do
less. He accepts us, not because of what we do for Him, but because
of what He's done for us in Christ. The Bible says, "He made us
accepted in the Beloved [that is, Jesus]" (Ephesians 1:6). And nothing "shall be able to separate us from the love of God which is in
Christ Jesus our Lord" (Romans 8:39). Love God, and within the
limitations He has sovereignly placed in your life at this time, do
what you can.

REMEMBER THE PHYSICALITY OF SPIRITUALITY

OUR BODIES ARE NOT MERELY DISPOSABLE CONTAINERS FOR OUR eternal souls. God could have made us to be disembodied souls, living forever in a condition like the souls in Heaven live while waiting for their resurrected bodies. Or He could have made us more like insects and animals, living bodies without eternal souls. But He created us to be complete as a unity of body and soul, and thus shall we be forever (even after the Lord's return and we have our resurrected bodies; see 1 Corinthians 15:35-58; 2 Corinthians 5:1-4).

One aspect of this relationship between body and soul is the effect our flesh and blood can sometimes have on our spirit. I call this the physicality of our spirituality. We can see this, for example, in the negative impact sleeplessness eventually has upon prayer.

One of the ways the body can have a positive effect upon the soul is through recreational physical activity. Because most spiritual practices are by definition *spiritual* and *not* very physical, if our daily work is mostly mental and sedentary then there's little diversity in the kind of stimuli we experience. And the monotony of that can lessen the impact of our spiritual practices. The variety that recreational physical activity provides to the brain cells and muscle fibers of a body may help to refresh the soul that dwells in it.

In a similar way, Winston Churchill understood this when he wrote of the need for hands-on activities by those whose daily occupation is primarily brain work:

> But reading and book-love in all their forms [as hobbies] suffer from one serious defect: they are too nearly akin to the ordinary daily round of the brain-worker to give that element of change and contrast essential to real relief. To restore psychic

equilibrium we should call into use those parts of the mind which direct both the eye and hand. Many men have found great advantage in practicing a handicraft for pleasure. Joinery, chemistry, book-binding, even bricklaying—if one were interested in them and skillful at them—would give a real relief to the over-tired brain. But, best of all and easiest to procure are sketching and painting in all their forms. I consider myself very lucky that late in life I have been able to develop this new taste and pastime.[1]

It's generally agreed that until Jesus was thirty, in addition to the time He obviously spent praying and learning the Bible, He worked with His hands in the family carpentry shop. The apostle Paul, though he received a first-rate education from his earliest years and earned the Ph.D. of his time, also learned to make tents along the way, and practiced the trade as necessary throughout his missionary labors. In addition, both men would have walked an average of several miles per week in the course of the spiritual work of the ministry and practicing their personal spiritual disciplines.

Find some physical activities that result in a "good tired," a fatigue that's natural and emptied of stress. Make sure that your life isn't all head and no hands. Learn to see how the right amount of the right kind of physical activity can improve your spirituality.

Take a Nap

Sometimes the most spiritual thing you can do is to take a nap. The average amount of sleep for Americans declined from more than nine hours per night in 1850 to seven hours in 1990.[2] Other studies verify what most of us know by experience, that many are operating with a serious "sleep debt." While it's true that both Jesus (see Luke 6:12) and the apostle Paul (see 2 Corinthians 6:5) occasionally were up all night for the sake of the kingdom of God, the Bible also tells us this about our heavenly Father: "He gives His beloved sleep" (Psalm 127:2).

God made us a unity of body and soul, and one influences the other. When your soul is either happy or discouraged, it can affect how your body looks and feels. And when your body is exhausted, it tends to dampen the zeal of your soul. In fact, fatigue often weakens our resolve against temptation and provides excuses for anger, lust, and other sins.

God made us to need sleep. Pastor and author John Piper once sat wearily on the side of his bed trying to develop a theology of sleep. After all, he reasoned, we could do so much more for God's kingdom if we didn't have to sleep nearly a third of our lives away. Eventually, John concluded, "Sleep is a daily reminder from God that we are not God."[3] We are neither omnipotent nor omnicompetent, and the need for sleep is a daily reminder of that. Every night we have to go to bed and leave things in the hands of God.

One word of warning: Don't sinfully neglect your spiritual disciplines and then talk about the need to get some "spiritual" sleep. It's one thing to occasionally be so tired from God-given responsibilities that you can't read the Bible or pray; it's another to be often distracted by "the cares of this world, the deceitfulness of riches, and the desires for other things" (Mark 4:19), and then claim weariness as an exemption from the disciplines.

The body needs sleep just as the soul needs communion with God. Sometimes what pleases Him most is when "His beloved" receives a nap as His gift.

Do Nothing — and Do It
to the Glory of God

THE BIBLE TELLS US, "THEREFORE, WHETHER YOU EAT OR DRINK, OR whatever you do, do all to the glory of God" (1 Corinthians 10:31). I suggest there are times when we should do *nothing*—and do it "to the glory of God."

One Sunday morning in my boyhood, I was waiting for my parents to finish dressing for church. "Hurry up," I complained from the family room. "I don't have anything else to do except sit here and think."

Somehow, as soon as the words left my mouth, I knew I was going to get an answer I didn't want to hear. Maybe that's why I still remember my dad's reply. "Sometimes," came his voice from down the hall, "it's good to just sit and think."

Unlike now, my life as an only child in a small, Mississippi River delta town in northeast Arkansas gave me many opportunities (besides waiting for my parents) to do nothing, to "just sit and think." Back then I considered most of that inactive time to be boring. Now I realize that in many ways those moments were the making of me. Undistracted and unhurried, I could think about everything from how God could be everywhere at the same time, to how to throw a curveball. And because I heard or read much about God and the gospel in church, my home, and my daily Bible reading, thoughts about the things of God had the time to root deeply into the soil of my soul. I also had time for my imagination to work.

My occasional need to imitate Rodin's statue *The Thinker* didn't disappear with my childhood. If anything, my information-overloaded brain needs daydream breaks now more than ever. Yours probably does too, so take time on occasion to do nothing — in the presence of God and to the glory of God. It will help simplify your spiritual life, for spirituality doesn't get any simpler than doing nothing.

LIVE BIBLICALLY ON THE LORD'S DAY

I ASSUME THAT ALMOST NO ONE READING THIS BOOK NEEDS TO BE persuaded to attend church.[4] Beyond your good habit of church attendance, however, how do you decide what else you should or should not do on Sunday?

When it comes to making such decisions, I understand there to be three major views among Christians. One is the *Christian Sabbath view*. This view says that the Fourth Commandment—"Remember the Sabbath day, to keep it holy . . . " (Exodus 20:8-11)—is a perpetual, moral law of God and remains intact under the New Covenant. Instead of a Saturday Sabbath as in the Old Covenant, Christians observe the Sabbath on Sunday in commemoration of the resurrection of Jesus Christ. Except for the ceremonial aspects of the Jewish Sabbath, all the other Sabbath laws should be embraced by Christians today, just as much as any of the other Ten Commandments.

The *Lord's Day view* points to texts like Colossians 2:16-17 and Hebrews 4:9-10, arguing that the Sabbath was "a shadow of things to come, but the substance is of Christ" (Colossians 2:17). Like the Day of Atonement, the Sabbath pointed to Christ. Jesus Christ is the true Sabbath. And when we rest from (that is, stop relying upon) our good works as the way to be right with God and rest by faith in the finished work of Christ on our behalf, we "keep the Sabbath" (or rather, Christ keeps it perfectly for us). Among those who take this view is a wide range of perspectives on what—in addition to public worship—it means to observe the Lord's Day.

However, most Christians apparently prefer a third position. I call it the *Oblivious view*. In other words, these believers go to church, but beyond that they've never considered whether the Bible has anything to say about what else they should or shouldn't do on Sunday. They make their decisions about these things based far more upon cultural influences than upon the Bible or anything else. The "culture" that influences their actions may be their church culture or the general culture, but the primary influence is culture nonetheless. If just about everyone in their church commonly shops for groceries or goes to the mall on Sunday afternoon, then they will probably feel comfortable doing the same themselves. And if most everyone in the culture at large seems to be watching football on Sunday, then they won't think twice about turning on the game after Sunday dinner.

I want to encourage you to base your decisions about your Lord's Day activities—whatever they may be—more intentionally upon the Bible. That's what a Christian really wants to do in everything, isn't it? It's also closer to true spirituality to acknowledge the authority of Scripture over how you spend your Sunday. Study the issue, be persuaded in your own mind, and then act accordingly. Believe that it's always more blessed by God and glorifying to God to choose to live biblically.

DELIGHT IN THE LORD'S DAY

WHAT'S THE FIRST THING THAT COMES TO MIND WHEN YOU HEAR the biblical term *Sabbath*? Many people, including those familiar with the New Testament, may think first of legalism. That's because nearly every mention of Sabbath in the Gospels has to do with the Pharisees accusing Jesus of violating their manmade rules. God's original intention, however, was for the Jews to "call the Sabbath a delight" (Isaiah 58:13). He meant for each of them on that day to "delight [themselves] in the LORD" (verse 14). Far from being a day to dread because of its restrictions, God designed the Sabbath to be a delightful day, the best of the week.

If that is true in the Old Testament, how much more should those who know God through Christ and have His Holy Spirit find delight in "the Lord's Day" (Revelation 1:10)?

How do we do this? As I mentioned in the previous chapter, there are differing views on what the Bible teaches about the Lord's Day. But those rooted deeply in Scripture would agree on at least these two principles (though some would argue for much more): First, our greatest privilege and most important responsibility on the Lord's Day is to worship Him with His people. Not only was the Old Testament Sabbath a day of worship, but we also have the apostolic command about "not forsaking the assembling of ourselves together" (Hebrews 10:25). And the apostolic example associated with this command is worship "on the first day of the week" (Acts 20:7; 1 Corinthians 16:2).

Second, all our activities on Sunday should reflect the fact that it is "the Lord's Day" (over and above the fact that, according to Psalm 118:24, *every* day is "the day the LORD has made"). As you would expect, the practical aspects of what this means are very personal and intensely debated. In general, I think it means devoting ourselves to the pursuit of those things that promote the enjoyment of God. This also includes those activities that edify our churches and families, extend the kingdom of God, and refresh our souls and bodies.

Years ago I began to delight in the Lord's Day much more intentionally. One change was to redirect the time I spent watching sports on TV on Sunday afternoons. It wasn't because I don't like watching sports anymore, for I enjoy that as much as ever. Rather, I stopped watching in order to turn to activities that would better restore my soul and recreate my body. People speak of "vegging" in front of the TV. Staring at a screen for hours may not make us more tired, but neither does it invigorate us. Unlike taking a nap or a prayer-walk, reading the Bible or other good book alone or with family, or having a time of spiritual fellowship with other believers, we don't feel refreshed after an afternoon of TV watching.

Imagine living to age seventy and spending every Lord's Day in the ways I've suggested. You'd experience ten years of worshiping the Lord with His people, reading great literature, playing with your children or grandchildren, taking walks, enjoying fellowship, and taking naps. Does this sound like a burden to you? Most people dream of a life like this. It's the kind of life you *can* enjoy when you delight in the Lord's Day.

Start Your Week by Stopping

The front-page headline of a recent issue of *USA Today* reads, "24/7 almost a way of life." The article begins with, "The nation has an unofficial new motto . . . 24/7. 24/7 isn't just an expression, it's a cultural earthquake that is changing the way we live."[5]

In times past we had to arrange our lives so we could shop and run errands before places closed. Now we have the "convenience" of shopping at increasing numbers of stores that stay open around the clock. We can get the latest news or find something interesting on TV twenty-four hours a day. Email piles up in our inbox day and night, and entire galaxies of useful websites wait to be explored in the ever-expanding universe of cyberspace. Partially because of such unprecedented opportunities provided by technology and prosperity, we also suffer with less sleep than any previous generation. Eventually, though, the need for sleep keeps us from staying busy a full twenty-four hours of every day.

But the "7" part of the 24/7 is another matter. Years ago the culture still provided a change of pace on Sunday. Few merchants opened their doors, which meant few people worked, little was bought and sold, and hardly any folks were scurrying around in order to go to work or to buy things. In general, everyone had a slower, simpler day than on other days. Today, almost nothing restrains us from being as busy on the Lord's Day as on the other six days of the week. Virtually everything available to us Monday through Saturday is available on Sunday. And for many Christians, other than church attendance and (perhaps) not going to work, Sunday is now no different from any other day.

That's a big reason why the lives of almost everyone seem so complex: in a 24/7 world there's no sense of when the week begins or ends. There's no longer a day when we *have* to stop. As a result, there's no more desperately needed way of simplifying the spiritual life of Christians today than delighting in the Lord's Day.

The Bible designates Sunday as "the first day of the week" (Matthew 28:1). Our week does have a beginning. And on that day we should enjoy a sense of closure to one week and the freshness of another. For that to happen, however, we must *choose* to stop. We must erect walls that hold back the unfinished backlog of life on one side and the appealing opportunities provided by technology and prosperity on the other, and live within that restful space for one day. And we must do it for the health of our souls and bodies, for the blessing of our families and relationships, and for the building of the church and the kingdom of God.

Let the world live 24/7; I want weeks with ends and beginnings. The Lord gave us an example when, after the "six days [in which] the LORD made the heavens and the earth . . . He rested" (Exodus 31:17). On the Lord's Day, let's delight in following His example.

SCHEDULE MARGIN ON THE LORD'S DAY

OTHER THAN THE BIBLE, THERE ARE FEW BOOKS I'VE READ TWICE. But I found Richard A. Swenson's *Margin* and *The Overload Syndrome* so helpful I've read them four times. Swenson warns that the inexorable roll of progress in technology and the economy tends to erode progress in the areas that matter most—our relationships with God and others. This erosion occurs, according to Swenson, because technological and economic "progress" influences us to live with less margin. Technological progress inevitably complicates life as it adds both to our responsibilities and to our choices for information and entertainment. Economic progress rarely results in more leisure; rather, it typically leads to more work and more debt, which leads to more pressure to work. And by always depleting our reserves, that is, by living *without* margin in the use of our bodies, emotions, money, and time, we eventually collapse in one or more of these areas.

Swenson recognizes that few people can immediately make the sweeping changes necessary to restore margin in every area of life. One place I believe many can—and need—to begin recovering margin is on the Lord's Day. Two ways to do this are to schedule freedom *from* some things and freedom *for* some things.

Schedule freedom from busywork. Though there's always plenty of it to do, avoid housework on the Lord's Day. Make it a day free from laundry, cleaning, polishing, home maintenance, and anything else that can possibly wait. The same goes for yard work, washing the car, cleaning out the garage, running errands, paying bills, organizing things, and anything tedious.

Schedule freedom from commerce. Try to live this one day without spending money, even via the Internet. Instead of buying and selling, focus on giving (primarily through your local church) and on the things in life that can't be bought and sold.

Schedule freedom from electronic communication and entertainment. Do you stare at a computer screen for much of your workday? Do you spend time on a typical weeknight in front of a TV? If so, then sending email, surfing the Internet, and watching TV on the Lord's Day make it much like every other day. On the first day of the week, take a break from the activities that dominate all other days.

Schedule freedom for the most important things in life. Take the time provided by the freedom from other things and devote it to the worship of God (our highest priority on the Lord's Day) and the work of His kingdom. Pursue, as much as possible, the replenishment of body and soul with rest, silence and solitude, and reading—especially of the Bible and other Christian literature—for which there seems to be such limited time during the week. Think, too, of the Lord's Day as a day for family togetherness—both with your immediate family and with your local church family.

When Jesus first visited the home of sisters Mary and Martha, Mary "sat at Jesus' feet and heard His word. But Martha was distracted with much serving." At last He said to her, "Martha, Martha, you are worried and troubled about many things. But one thing is needed, and Mary has chosen that good part, which will not be taken away from her" (Luke 10:39-42). On the Lord's Day, schedule freedom *from* being like Martha, and freedom *for* being like Mary. Start your week with margin, not exhaustion.

SIMPLIFYING
AND
OTHERS

Simplify Family Worship

A MAN WHO IS LIKE A SPIRITUAL FATHER TO ME BEGAN WHAT HE called a "family altar" with his wife before they were married and has faithfully continued the practice through the arrival of children and grandchildren for more than fifty years. Sadly, it seems that few men among even the best evangelical churches today could speak of daily family worship in their home. In the minds of some, active church involvement eliminates the need for family worship. For others, Bible reading, prayer, and singing praises to God together as a family have been crowded out by the TV, the Internet, and a nonstop schedule that makes even meals together a rarity.

But the father (and in his absence, the mother) of the family has the responsibility from God to provide spiritual leadership for his household. As He did with Abraham, the Lord wants every father to "command his children and his household after him, that they keep the way of the LORD" (Genesis 18:19). Each one should raise his children "in the training and admonition of the Lord" (Ephesians 6:4). Every husband should love his wife as Christ loves His bride — the church — and follow Christ's example of washing his wife with "the washing of water by the word" of God (Ephesians 5:26).

While it isn't the only way, the simplest method of applying all these texts in a steady, practical way is through daily family worship. This is how generations of Christians have understood them. For instance, both Baptists and Presbyterians in the 1600s saw this biblical teaching and incorporated identical language about the expectation of family worship into the most influential confessional statements in their respective histories. To this day, many churches still maintain (at least officially) that "God is to be worshipped everywhere in spirit and truth; as in private families daily."[1]

Somehow, though, many men have gotten the idea that family worship is complicated or that it requires time-consuming preparation. But it need not require any more preparation than your personal worship of God. And the entire experience can be reduced to three simple elements: read, pray, sing.

Read. The centerpiece of family worship is the Bible. Read a passage of appropriate length for your family, making any impromptu comments that come to mind. Those with younger children should emphasize the narrative portions of Scripture and possibly the Proverbs. Eventually, most seem to work up to about a chapter a day, reading consecutively through a particular book of the Bible. I recommend that you ask a few questions to determine comprehension, or just ask the children to repeat what they remember.

Pray. Let the words of the passage you read suggest matter for prayer. The husband/father should pray, and perhaps one or all the rest of the family members. Most days this will be brief.

Sing. Use a hymnal and sing *a cappella,* or sing along to a recording, or let a family musician lead the way. Sing as little as one verse or for as long as the family enjoys it.

Any order of "read, pray, sing" is fine. It doesn't have to be long to be effective. Be patient with the interest and attention span of the younger ones. Remember that you're not only fulfilling a responsibility to God by leading family worship, you're also introducing your children to Him. In these moments together, your children can see your love for God and for His Word, and some of the most teachable moments of their childhood will occur.

So start family worship in your home today. It doesn't matter when you have worship. For some, early morning is best. For others, it's mealtime, and for still others, it's bedtime. Just start. Whether you've been married fifty years or are newly engaged, just start. Keep it simple, and keep it up.

Leave a Spiritual Inheritance

"A good man," says Proverbs 13:22, "leaves an inheritance to his children's children." Leaving a material and financial inheritance in a wise manner is good stewardship and can be a great blessing to your heirs. But have you considered ways to leave an inheritance to your family that will have a more direct spiritual impact on them?

These spiritual lives we're trying to simplify aren't lived for ourselves only. We also bear responsibility to influence others spiritually, especially the members of our own families. To that end, here are a few items to leave as spiritual time capsules with prayers that they will bless many generations of your descendants.

Prayers. The beloved old Bible commentator Matthew Henry said somewhere that wise parents are more concerned about leaving a treasury of prayers for their children than a treasury of silver and gold. Long after we are dead, God can answer the prayers for our children and future generations we bring to His throne today. King Hezekiah's wicked son, Manasseh, repented and turned to the Lord many decades after Hezekiah died (see 2 Chronicles 33:12-19), but no doubt the father left behind a rich inheritance of prayers to God for his wayward boy. You may want to preserve some of your prayers for your descendants in letters or journals.

Journals. One hundred years from now, quite possibly all that will be known of you will be from photographs or videos, and from what you write. Despite your decades of life and labor, few, if any, of even your direct descendants a century from today will know anything about your spirituality. (What do you know about the inner life of your ancestors who, just 1,200 months ago, were as alive as you are now?) Leave your heirs a clear, written testimony of how you came to know God through Jesus Christ. Provide them with a record of answers to prayer, remarkable providences, significant spiritual events, and other works of God in your part of their family history. Write letters to your descendants, urging them to trust Christ, to maintain a Christian heritage in the family, and to meet you in Heaven. Make a list of books that have influenced you.

Books. Leave a library—especially of Christian books—for your children and their children. The Lord may use the books to bring them to Christ and to give solid guidance to their spiritual lives long after you are gone. Collect good books for your children or grandchildren even before they are born. I've always bought books (both Christian and general reading) for my daughter, Laurelen, years before she could enjoy them. In fact, I started buying books for her future children when she was just six years old. So if I find a bargain on boys' books, I'll buy them—even though Laurelen will probably never read them—in anticipation of having grandsons someday. Who knows whether some of the great old used books I find for them today will still be available or affordable by then?

Daily planners. If you have the space, archive your daily planners. These reflect how you've spent your time and, combined with your journals, provide a fairly complete biography of your adult life.

Of course, your most immediate spiritual legacy is the life you live before the watching eyes of your children and grandchildren. However, some (all?) of your grandchildren or great-grandchildren may never know you personally. But if you leave them a rich spiritual inheritance, they may say of you, "He being dead still speaks" (Hebrews 11:4).

READ BOOKS TO YOUR FAMILY
THAT STIMULATE SPIRITUALITY

I WRITE THIS CHAPTER WITH THE ASSUMPTION THAT YOU APPRECI-
ate the importance of reading to your children. I advocate this
practice for as long as your children will endure it (even into
adulthood), as well as reading to your spouse even if you have no
children.

When you do read to your family, make it more than just good
family time by reading books that will stimulate spirituality—both
yours and theirs. I don't mean that you necessarily have to read
books with explicitly Christian subject matter. Rather, I mean to
encourage two things.

First, read well-written books to your family. C. S. Lewis said,
"No book is really worth reading at the age of ten which is not
equally (and often far more) worth reading at the age of fifty." Also,
"a children's story which is enjoyed only by children is a bad children's story."² Books enjoyed by all ages invariably deal with univer-
sal, enduring themes. Children who show little interest in family
Bible reading (which is indispensable in a Christian home) will pay
attention to a well-told tale.

That leads to my second point: Take advantage of teachable
moments that occur while reading to the family. A wise reader can
always relate great stories to the teaching of Scripture. In fact, doing
this would be one of the easiest ways to apply the famous instructions to parents in Deuteronomy 6:6-7: "And these words which I
command you today shall be in your heart. You shall teach them
diligently to your children, and shall talk of them when you sit in
your house, when you walk by the way, when you lie down, and
when you rise up."

Whether it's by means of something like Lewis's own classic *Chronicles of Narnia* books or a more overtly Christian standard like John Bunyan's *Pilgrim's Progress,* read books that will edify as well as entertain.

Sing the Table Blessing

WHEN I WAS A CHILD, MY CHRISTIAN PARENTS ASSIGNED TO ME THE mealtime responsibility of thanking the Lord for our food and of asking His blessing upon it. They never required me to vary the few words I prayed, so before long the thrice-daily habit devolved into mechanical repetition. One time I went through the ritual so mindlessly that instead of starting by saying, "Dear heavenly Father," I crossed wires with my phone answering routine and began my prayer with "Hello?"

The traditional Christian practice of thanking God for food dates to biblical times. Jesus "gave thanks" to the Father for the loaves and fishes before He miraculously multiplied the food to feed thousands (Matthew 15:36). It was after "He had given thanks" that He distributed the bread at the last supper with His disciples (1 Corinthians 11:24). The book of Acts records that the apostle Paul "took bread and gave thanks to God" (27:35), and in 1 Timothy 4:3-5 he taught us to do likewise.

No one wants to bore or be bored when giving thanks to God in prayer. But when we thank Him for the same thing (our food) every few hours more than a thousand times a year, year after year, it's easy to find ourselves praying on autopilot (a practice Jesus condemns as "vain repetitions" in Matthew 6:7). Singing the table blessing can refresh the routine.

Where to begin? In one brief search I found several Internet pages devoted to this subject. Each posted lyrics and suggested familiar tunes. With very little effort you could bring one to the table with you on occasion. But you may prefer to create your own, perhaps adapting one or more verses of Scripture. A child taking music lessons might enjoy composing a short tune for musical thanks that's unique to your family. Or during a mealtime or two you could develop a table blessing as a family project.

Like any other method, a table blessing that's sung can also become a mindless routine if it's repeated without variety. Used wisely, however, singing your thanks to the Lord at mealtime can adorn the commonplace with a touch of simple beauty.

Ask People How You Can Pray for Them

Over and over I've seen one simple question open people's hearts to hear the gospel. Until I asked this question, they showed no interest in spiritual matters. But then after six words—only seventeen letters in English—I've seen people suddenly begin to weep and their resistance fall. The question is, "How can I pray for you?"

This may not seem like such a powerful question to you. Perhaps that's because you hear it, or a question like it, quite often. Your Bible study group or your church prayer meeting asks for prayer requests every week. You may even see requests for prayer solicited each Sunday morning in the worship bulletin.

But realize that most people in the world *never* hear such a question. And while many churchgoers know that a minister is willing to pray for them, in some traditions they're expected to make a special donation to the church for such services. So when you ask, "How can I pray for you?" and it's obvious that you're asking out of love alone, it can touch a person more deeply than you imagine.

This question is similar to one that Jesus Himself sometimes asked: "What do you want Me to do for you?" (Matthew 20:32). For what we are really asking is, "What do you want me to ask Jesus to do for you?" And by means of this question, we can show the love of Christ to people and open hearts previously closed to the gospel.

I had tried to talk about the things of God many times to a business-hardened, retired executive who lived next door. He was a pro at hiding his feelings and keeping conversations at a superficial level. But the day we stood between our homes and I asked, "How can I pray for you?" his eyes filled with tears as his façade of self-sufficiency melted. For the first time in seven years he let me speak with him about Jesus.

It's a short, easily remembered question. You can use it with longtime friends or with people you've just met. It doesn't seem too personal or pushy for those who'd rather give you a shallow answer just then, and yet it often leads to a full hearing of the gospel. You can ask it of people nearly every time you speak with them and it doesn't get old. Just simply and sincerely ask, "How can I pray for you?" You'll be surprised at the results.

Prepare for Evangelism
with a Simple Outline

MANY CHRISTIANS THINK THEY CANNOT ADEQUATELY SHARE THE gospel unless they've had formal training in evangelism. I'm for evangelism training, but training is not necessary before you can tell someone about Jesus and give your own testimony about how you came to know Him.

In John 9 we read of a man born blind who, within an hour after his conversion, is witnessing to Ph.D.s in religion (the Pharisees). Obviously, he'd had no evangelism training, but he was able to talk about Jesus and his own conversion. As Martyn Lloyd-Jones used to say, after being saved and after hearing countless presentations of the gospel in sermons, if Christians still believe they cannot evangelize without massive amounts of training, then either they've heard very poor preaching or they've been very poor listeners.

However, it does boost one's confidence in sharing the gospel to know a general outline of what to say and to have some appropriate verses of Scripture committed to memory. Several years ago I developed an outline to hang my thoughts on, along with at least two key verses for each section. I don't follow it woodenly in every situation, for each evangelistic encounter is unique. And sometimes I condense it a bit. But having a full presentation of the gospel ready on my lips does give me a sense of direction and a feeling of preparedness. You're welcome to adapt the outline for use in your own personal evangelism.

1. There is one God, He is the Creator, He is holy, and He is worth knowing. See Deuteronomy 4:39; Isaiah 46:9; Genesis 1:1; 1 Peter 1:16. Such a God is worthy of our pursuit!

2. Everyone is a sinner separated from God. See Romans 3:23; Isaiah 59:2. We have no idea how unholy we are in comparison to God.

3. There is a penalty for sin. See Romans 6:23; Hebrews 9:27; Romans 14:10; Matthew 25:46. The penalty is judgment and Hell.

4. Jesus paid that penalty for all who believe. See Romans 5:8; 1 Peter 3:18. Jesus took God's judgment so believers could have mercy.

5. No one can earn God's forgiveness and favor. See Ephesians 2:8-9; Titus 3:5. We're not saved by our works, but by faith in Jesus' work.

6. We should respond with repentance and faith. See Mark 1:15; John 3:16. We should turn from sin and turn to Jesus for forgiveness.

7. We can have assurance of eternal life with God. See 1 John 5:13. Jesus' resurrection and God's Word assure believers of forgiveness.

Responding to this great message from the Bible.

A. It is not only right for you to live for the God who created you and owns you, but you will find your greatest fulfillment only when you fulfill the purpose for which you were made, and that is to know God and live for Him.

B. Do you believe this great message of the Bible? Genuine belief in its truth is demonstrated by turning from living for yourself and believing that because of His death and resurrection Jesus Christ can make you right with God.

C. Are you willing to express repentance and faith in prayer to God right now?

Serve Effectively

THOSE WHO HAVE "THE SPIRIT OF CHRIST" (ROMANS 8:9) LIVING within them will, like Christ, love His church and want to serve God through the church. Most servants of God, however, find that this compulsion to serve must be expressed within the limits of a hectic and stressful life. In other words, the *time* available to serve God in and through His church never seems equal to our *desire* to serve Him.

Service to God is worth the sacrifices necessary to make it a priority. Still, the limits of time require that we choose *how* and *where* to strengthen our local church. So any simplifying of the spiritual life should include evaluating whether the ways we now serve are the most effective ways.

One way to serve effectively is in a ministry in which you can *use your spiritual gift*. Whenever the Spirit of God indwells a believer, He bestows a spiritual gift, "distributing to each one individually as He wills" (1 Corinthians 12:11). This gift is a God-created desire and power for a particular kind of ministry within the body of Christ. (Lists of these gifts may be found in Romans 12:6-8; 1 Corinthians 12:4-11,28-30; and Ephesians 4:7-13.) Ministering within the areas of your giftedness will produce the most satisfying, fruitful, and enthusiastic service.

Evaluate your current activity (or inactivity) afresh in light of your spiritual gift and consider the full range of ministry opportunities available to you in your church. Think, too, of new ministries you could initiate (see the next chapter). Even if you aren't sure which spiritual gift you have, concentrate the bulk of your ministry time in areas where you *think* your heart and abilities best belong. Theologian J. I. Packer reminds us, "The most significant gifts in the church's life in every era are ordinary natural abilities sanctified."[3]

That leads to a second way of maximizing your ministry effectiveness: Serve where the church body hurts. Granted, there are times when some church ministries should be allowed to shrink or even disappear, despite their cries for help. Frequently, however, some of the most important ministries within a church suffer needlessly for a lack of workers. By itself, the existence of a need does not constitute the call of God for you to fill it. But sometimes the hurts within the local body of Christ reflect nothing more than the unwillingness of its members to serve selflessly for Christ's kingdom and God's glory.

God does not *need* our service, of course. If He chooses, He can accomplish whatever He pleases without us. Yet it is our great privilege to serve Him in His church. All the glory of our service is His too. For even the desire and the strength to serve is from Him, because "it is God who works in you both to will and to do for His good pleasure" (Philippians 2:13). "Whoever serves is to do so as one who is serving by the strength which God supplies; so that in all things God may be glorified through Jesus Christ" (1 Peter 4:11, NASB).

"Serve the LORD with gladness" (Psalm 100:2, NASB), and serve Him effectively.

Invent a Ministry

THE LAWSONS WORK HARD ALL WEEK LONG. MICHAEL'S JOB USUALLY requires much more than a forty-hour weekly commitment. Susan never imagined such a busy life. And while their children aren't over-involved, just a couple of school, sports, or music activities per week by each of them put many extra miles on the family van almost every afternoon and evening. The Lawsons spend most of the rest of their time trying to catch up with "life maintenance"—housework, shopping, paying bills, yard work, running errands, and all the rest. They almost always feel behind or overwhelmed.

And yet, like all those indwelled by the Spirit of Christ, they love what Christ loves—the church. They genuinely want to serve the Lord in and through His church. They have a good sense of the biblical priorities in life, but they struggle with what often seem to be *too many* priorities. They don't want to be mere religious consumers at church. Instead they want to minister and to do so in a way that glorifies God, strengthens the church, provides an example to their children, and edifies themselves. With everything else going on in their lives at this time, and with the limited options for ministry at their church, what should they do?

Some in this situation could find a solution to their problem just by talking with their pastor about it. He probably knows of opportunities for service invisible to many church members. Moreover, he's certain to have ideas for ministries the church could begin if only the workers appeared.

For many people, a simple, creative solution is to invent a ministry. Perhaps the Lord has allowed the current circumstances just so the Lawsons and people like them would look in new directions and begin some much-needed, but previously unconsidered, ministry.

This is similar to what happened in Acts 6:1-7 when a situation developed that prompted the church's leadership to invent a ministry to meet a growing need.

While most churches need workers in existing ministries, the inability to fit well in one of them may be God's prompting to start a new one. It doesn't necessarily have to be a formally recognized ministry. It could be as simple as providing transportation for someone who's blind, feeble, or without a car. Or it might be showing up extra early just to be available where needed.

If the idea of inventing a new ministry appeals to you, begin by asking the Lord to show you the answer to these two questions: "What are the greatest needs inside the church?" and "What are the church's greatest needs for outreach?" By guiding your recollection, observation, or the comments of others, I'm confident He'll lead you.

The Bible says, "Let us not grow weary while doing good" (Galatians 6:9). Why is this in the Scriptures? Because for so many reasons we *do* get tired while doing good. Like Jesus, let us never give up on His church or its work, no matter how tired or busy we become. Dream of new ways to use the gifts, skills, resources, and desires God has given you in imaginative and fulfilling ways in your church. It could simplify the public part of your spiritual life.

Seek True Fellowship,
Not Mere Socializing

"We have such good fellowship at our church," she said.

"That's great," I replied, "but how do you know?"

"Because so many people linger after the services to talk."

Well, what occurs between people after the service might be fellowship, but it might be mere socializing. Socializing (such as talking about the news, weather, work, or other matters) is a good part of life, but socializing is not the same as fellowship. Unbelievers can socialize; only Christians can truly fellowship. But far too often we think we've enjoyed the rich feast of fellowship when we've only snacked on sometimes tasty but spiritually empty socializing.

At its simple best, fellowship involves two or more Holy Spirit-indwelled people talking about God and the things of God. But we do this far less than we imagine. Think—when was the last time you had a spiritually stimulating conversation with another believer? And yet the Christians in the book of Acts were so devoted to fellowship with each other that in the first description of the activities of the first church only their listening to the apostles preach and teach is listed ahead of it (see Acts 2:42).

A significant part of the Lord's ministry to us comes through others in whom He lives. And He intends for us to experience much of this comforting, encouraging, instructing, reproving, guiding, and sustaining ministry through fellowship. But if we talk with our brothers and sisters almost exclusively about things even worldlings can discuss and understand, we deprive ourselves of many touches from Heaven.

True fellowship seldom occurs unintentionally, especially among those who do not yet see the difference between fellowship and socializing. Enjoy socializing with other Christians, but discipline yourself to talk more about things that matter, and talk about them as though they *do* matter.

CULTIVATE *KOINONIA*

THE WORD *FELLOWSHIP* IN THE NEW TESTAMENT (AS IN ACTS 2:42) is a translation of the Greek word *koinonia*. At its root, *koinonia* describes two or more people in close association and often speaks of these people as sharing in something, such as a marriage or business. Christian *koinonia* exists between everyone who knows God through Jesus Christ (see 1 John 1:3). Everyone united with Christ by faith is also united with everyone else united with Christ. The same Holy Spirit indwells all believers and gives each a common share in the body of Christ, the church. As the apostle Paul put it, "For by one Spirit we were all baptized into one body . . . and have all been made to drink into one Spirit" (1 Corinthians 12:13).

The presence of the Holy Spirit in each other enables Christian relationships to be enriched with a supernatural dimension and spiritual dynamic that unbelievers cannot experience. For example, the Lord Himself blesses us through the words of other Spirit-indwelled people in ways He seldom does through Spirit-less people. The easiest and most direct way to experience these blessings of *koinonia* is just to talk with another believer about the things of God. This includes anything related to knowing God, Christian living, understanding the Bible and applying it to particular issues such as work or family or culture, prayer, theology, church, and evangelism.

But as normal as such fellowship should be to those who know Christ, if we don't cultivate it, *koinonia* gets choked out of our conversations by the weeds of words about other things. Many Christians seem almost as reluctant to initiate a discussion about spiritual things with another believer as they are with an unbeliever. Just as we often do with unbelievers, we suppose, *They don't want to talk about God now,* or *They'll think I'm weird,* or *They'll think I'm try-*

ing to be super-spiritual. So we sigh and chat of other things instead, even though our hearts ache for more satisfying interaction with our Christian brothers and sisters.

One simple way to cultivate *koinonia* is to ask questions designed to turn a conversation in a more spiritual direction. Here's a list to work from:

1. How is your [teaching, hospitality, outreach, deacon, or whatever] ministry going? What do you enjoy most about it?
2. Where have you seen the Lord at work lately?
3. What's the Lord been teaching you recently?
4. Have you had any evangelistic opportunities lately?
5. Have you had any obvious answers to prayer recently?
6. What have you been reading? How has it impressed you?
7. Where in the Bible have you been reading lately? What impact has it had on you?
8. How can I pray for you?
9. What's the growth point in your life right now?
10. What are you passionate about right now?

You may want to write these down and put the list in your daily planner or your wallet, or enter them into a file to access electronically. You may prefer to develop other questions of your own. But don't wait for someone else to initiate *koinonia*—be prepared to cultivate it.

Cultivate *Koinonia* in the Church

We should cultivate *koinonia* (that is, fellowship — satisfy-ing conversation between believers about the things of God) when-ever possible wherever we encounter another believer. But the local church is the *primary* place to seek fellowship. That's not to say that *koinonia* should be confined within the walls of a church building. Rather, your local church *family* is the circle of relationships designed by God in which to feast your soul on *koinonia* most often. Acts 2:42 says that fellowship (the English translation of the Greek word *koinonia*) was one of the four most prominent characteristics of the New Testament church in its formative days. Like those believers, we should work to make *koinonia* a priority in our churches too.

Some churches don't need any more of what I call "sit and lis-ten" meetings, where only one person speaks and everyone else lis-tens. The greatest need of the church today *does* have to do with "sit and listen" meetings, however. The church needs men of God filled with the Spirit of God preaching the Word of God even more than it needs good fellowship. In fact, in Acts 2:42 the priority position was given to the proclamation of Scripture, not to fellowship. But in some churches where the authority of Scripture has been properly recovered there is an *over*correction that neglects *koinonia*. Both ministers and laymen should consider how to structure the min-istries of the church and how to conduct the meetings of the church in ways that will result in more opportunities for true fellowship.

For example, ministers could transform part of some church gatherings (not during Sunday morning worship, in most cases) where people could ask questions about the most recent sermon(s) or other spiritual matters. Perhaps a regular meeting of the church could include time where anyone could give a prayer request or testimony, or say anything else that might be of interest to the church. I know of several churches where the ministers lead a monthly get-together in one or more homes (often on Sunday night) that thrives on questions and discussions about recent sermons and all other questions people have about the Bible, Christian living, books they've read, and so forth. The staff in larger churches, of course, would have to modify these suggestions. All such *koinonia* is increasingly important in a situation where most church members never see anyone else from church any other time except *at* church.

Church member, take the initiative to cultivate *koinonia* within your own sphere of influence in the church. Even if your church has no meetings devoted to true fellowship, you can take advantage of any leadership responsibilities you have in a Bible study class, a small group, a committee, or some other ministry to cultivate *koinonia* there. For the better the *koinonia,* the better the church. Do your part to help the church function in the way the Lord ordained.

Fellowship Face to Face, Part 1

I SENT AND READ DOZENS OF EMAILS TODAY. IN ADDITION TO THE Internet contacts with people I had here in my own city and country, I heard from a pastor in Wales, exchanged several posts with a friend in Canada, and bought an old fountain pen from a woman in Germany through an online auction. What a great blessing to enjoy these things so easily. But as a result of the time involved at the computer, I haven't talked face to face with anyone all day. Why does it seem that the more I have and the faster I can accomplish things, the more distant I feel from people?

Because of the efficiency and convenience provided by technology, we chat and buy more and more through electronic means, but less and less in person. As long as we maintain meaningful face-to-face relationships, especially with fellow Christians, then our electronic relationships will remain in a good and healthy place. But if we interact with people *primarily* through glass or some sort of technological screen—such as a TV or computer monitor—we shouldn't be surprised that our relationships begin to seem distant, shallow, or artificial.

Even from the low-tech times of the first century, the timeless words of the Bible speak directly to this contemporary problem. Notice how the apostle John acknowledged the superiority of face-to-face fellowship over written communication: "I had many things to write, but I do not wish to write to you with pen and ink; but I hope to see you shortly, and we shall speak face to face" (3 John 13-14). While John used and clearly valued the written word, he would not let that substitute for what can be communicated only in the intimacy of Christian fellowship.

Similarly, Eugene Peterson observes that "words can be put into two piles: words used for communication and words used for communion. Words used for communion are the words used to tell stories, to make love, nurture intimacies, develop trust. Words used for communication are used to buy stocks, sell cauliflower, direct traffic, teach algebra."[4] While both piles of words are necessary, the words of communion—the words that nurture Christian fellowship—are best spoken face to face. Don't let the explosive increase in the means of communication keep you from *personal* communion with other believers. For to the degree that our communication diminishes our communion, we lose something that's part of the essence of Christianity.

FELLOWSHIP FACE TO FACE, PART 2

UNTIL WELL INTO THE TWENTIETH CENTURY, MOST RELATIONSHIPS existed within a short distance—perhaps even a short walk—from home. Contact with friends, family, church members, merchants, and others typically happened face to face and took place in stable communities. Today we can do much of our job, communicate with friends and family, bank, shop, buy gas, and pay bills, and never come within shouting distance of another human being. Because of our increased mobility, we live so far from the people we do see at work and church that we never see them any other place or time. We can't pretend this has had no effect on relationships, including fellowship between Christians.

What can we do? First, recognize what's happening. With all its benefits, one of the special challenges of our age is learning to adapt to a world where everyday contact with real people is diminishing. Technology has brought far-flung friends and family closer to us, yet it doesn't bring them close enough. We can read or hear their words, but we cannot shake their hand, kiss their cheek, or sit beside them and talk. Technology even permits us to have frequent contact with strangers, but it can estrange us from those nearest to us.

Recognize not only the tendencies of technology to separate us, but also how relationships weaken when urban sprawl and thickening traffic increase driving time and stress. Once home, and the drawbridge of the garage door closes us into our castle, just the thought of hurrying off again and driving several miles—even though to gather with other believers—is often too exhausting too consider.

Second, resist the socially centrifugal forces that push us apart. Beware the temptation to sit at the computer or engage in electronic chats at the expense of face-to-face fellowship. We shouldn't be content merely to *watch* relationships and begin to "know" the people on TV better than our nearest neighbors or almost anyone in our church family.

Third, understand that such resistance probably requires being more intentional about face-to-face Christian fellowship. Participate in the aspects of church life that involve more than just sitting and listening. Don't rush off after church events. Linger and talk, especially about the things of God. Eat together with other church members whenever possible. Look for ways to have people from church in your home every month or two.

Hebrews 10:25 is a timeless and God-inspired reminder to maintain some simplicity about getting together with believers. Like the original recipients of this letter, we also need the basic exhortation about "not forsaking the assembling of ourselves together, as is the manner of some." It was the pressure of persecution that tempted the first readers of these words to give up gathering with other believers. Technology, distance, and the pace of life are more likely causes for isolating ourselves from other believers today. But our God-given need to meet with Christian people face to face and the God-glorifying purposes of such gatherings remain unchanged by time or culture.

Minimize Electronic Spirituality, Part 2

I FOUND A WEBSITE RECENTLY THAT PROMOTED ITSELF AS AN "online church." It claimed to provide opportunities for worship and fellowship, "just like a local church." Such "churches" position themselves perfectly for current trends, according to *American Demographics,* for "approximately 16 percent of teens say they will find a substitute for church experiences online within the next five years. Net spirituality is already the choice of 10 percent of nonChristians and 14 percent of Christians."[5]

Electronic spirituality is the use of resources like a computer or the Internet for the sake of the soul. Some Christians practice electronic spirituality primarily to enhance their individual devotional lives while others do so to connect with other Christians and to develop their interpersonal spirituality. In part 1, I addressed the former. Here I want to address my concerns about the latter and in particular the attempts of believers to experience the congregational spiritual disciplines of fellowship and worship online.

Let's think first about online worship. While watching a church worship service may be a blessing for those who cannot attend, watching worship can never replace the experience of assembling and participating with other worshipers. Online worship produces observers of worship, not participants. The spirit of worship in Scripture is not, "Let's watch worship," but "I was glad when they said to me, 'Let us *go* into the house of the LORD,'" and "Oh, magnify the LORD with me, and let us exalt His name *together"* (Psalm 122:1; 34:3, emphasis added).

Those few who do actually worship simultaneously while watching online still remain separated from the spiritual experiences that only those present can enjoy. Like couples who have been married online while watching each other on a computer monitor, the congregational worship of God without the presence of others just isn't the same experience. Besides, the temptation to do other things during the slower parts of the service or sermon, like checking email during the offering, distracts the online observer in ways that would never occur to those immersed in the actual worship gathering.

The blessings of Christian fellowship cannot be successfully digitized either. While we can benefit from a *kind* of fellowship with other Christians via the Internet, the exchange of nothing but disembodied words makes it only a kind of half-fellowship. I thank God for the technology that enables me to stay in touch so easily with fellow believers I know around the world, but that's not all the Christian contact I need. Fellowship that is only electronic and never personal is not true fellowship.

The apostle John was inspired to tell us, "We know that we have passed from death to life, because we love the brethren" (1 John 3:14). In other words, one of the ways we gain assurance of our salvation is by measuring the strength of our love for our Christian brothers and sisters. And like any other real love, this love cannot be content—no matter how many emails it receives—to love only at a digital distance, for there are some aspects of Christian fellowship you just can't download.

DISCUSSION GUIDE

THERE ARE SEVERAL WAYS TO USE THIS GUIDE TO STUDY *SIMPLIFY Your Spiritual Life* in a small group. You could study one of the eight sections of the book per group session. Another way is to make two sessions out of the longer sections, that is, the ones on First Principles, the Truth, Time, and Others, for a total of twelve sessions. A third approach is simply to take whatever chapters you want per session and discuss the book at your own pace. In any case, each of the following questions can be used in each session.

- What did you find most helpful in these chapters?
- What questions did these chapters raise for you?
- What did you disagree with?
- How has something in these chapters simplified your spiritual life?
- What are the implications of these chapters for our corporate spirituality?
- What was left unsaid in these chapters that should be added?
- What unstated links or relationships do you see between any of these chapters?
- How would the practice of these things bring glory to God? Make us more like Christ?
- How can some of these suggestions be applied in other situations, such as in family, work, or church?
- What surprised you in these chapters?

NOTES

Simplifying and First Principles

1. H. Norman Wright, *Simplify Your Life* (Wheaton, Ill.: Tyndale, 1998), p. 181.
2. Jean Fleming, *Between Walden and the Whirlwind* (Colorado Springs, Colo.: NavPress, 1985), p. 23.
3. Martin Luther, *Luther's Works*, vol. 31, Jaroslav Jan Pelikan, Hilton C. Oswald and Helmut T. Lehmann, eds. (Philadelphia: Fortress Press, 1999), CD-ROM edition.
4. For more on this, see John Owen, "The Grace and Duty of Being Spiritually Minded," *The Works of John Owen*, vol. 7 (1850–53; reprint, Edinburgh: The Banner of Truth Trust, 1965), pp. 262-497.
5. For more on the personal spiritual disciplines, see Donald S. Whitney, *Spiritual Disciplines for the Christian Life* (Colorado Springs, Colo.: NavPress, 1996), and *Spiritual Disciplines Within the Church* (Chicago: Moody, 1996) for more on the spiritual disciplines we practice with others.
6. Richard A. Swenson, *Margin* (Colorado Springs, Colo.: NavPress, 1992, 1995), p. 30.
7. Richard A. Swenson, *The Overload Syndrome* (Colorado Springs, Colo.: NavPress, 1998), pp. 43-44.
8. *Margin*, p. 30.
9. *The Overload Syndrome*, p. 44.
10. *Margin*, p. 34.
11. *Margin*, p. 35.
12. Quoted in *Margin*, p. 37.

Simplifying and the Truth

1. See the pertinent subsections of chapters 2 and 3 in Donald S. Whitney, *Spiritual Disciplines for the Christian Life* (Colorado Springs, Colo.: NavPress, 1991) as well as the chapters in this book "Ask the Joseph Hall Questions," "Ask the Philippians 4:8 Questions," and "Meditate and Apply."
2. U. Milo Kaufman, *The Pilgrim's Progress and Traditions in Puritan Meditation* (New Haven and London: Yale University Press, 1966), p. 123.
3. Thomas Wilson, *Rule of Reason*, London, 1553.

Simplifying and Prayer

1. Roger Steer, comp., *Spiritual Secrets of George Müller* (Wheaton, Ill.: Harold Shaw, 1985), pp. 61-62.

2. Arthur Bennett, ed., *The Valley of Vision: A Collection of Puritan Prayers and Devotions* (Edinburgh: The Banner of Truth Trust, 1975).
3. Bennett, p. 42.
4. Bennett, p. ix.
5. Joseph Hall, *The Art of Divine Meditation,* in *The Fifty Greatest Christian Classics,* vol. 3 (1607; reprint ed., Lafayette, Ind.: Sovereign Grace Trust Fund, 1990), p. 432.
6. Roger Steer, comp., *Spiritual Secrets of George Müller* (Wheaton, Ill.: Harold Shaw, 1985), pp. 61-62.
7. Francesca Premoli-Droulers, *Writers' Houses* (New York: The Vendome Press, 1995).
8. Jill Krementz, *The Writer's Desk* (New York: Random House, 1996).
9. Frank E. Gaebelein, gen. ed., *The Expositor's Bible Commentary,* vol. 5, *Proverbs* by Allen P. Ross (Grand Rapids, Mich.: Zondervan, 1991), pp. 1002-1003.

Simplifying and Your Journal
1. For more on this subject, see the chapter "Journaling . . . for the Purpose of Godliness" in Donald S. Whitney, *Spiritual Disciplines for the Christian Life* (Colorado Springs, Colo.: NavPress, 1991).
2. Tony Buzan, *The Mind Map Book* (New York: Dutton, 1996).
3. M. A. Noll, "George Whitefield," in *Evangelical Dictionary of Theology,* 2nd ed., Walter A. Elwell, ed., (Grand Rapids, Mich.: Baker Academic, 2001), p. 1273.
4. Arnold Dallimore, *George Whitefield: The Life and Times of the Great Evangelist of the Eighteenth-Century Revival* (Westchester, Ill.: Crossway Books, 1979), vol. 1, p. 80.
5. Jonathan Edwards, *The Works of Jonathan Edwards,* rev. Edward Hickman (1834; reprint, Edinburgh: The Banner of Truth Trust, 1974), vol. 1, p. xxiv.

Simplifying and Your Mind
1. Wendell Berry, *The Gift of Good Land* (San Francisco: North Point Press, 1981), p. 156.
2. Bobb Biehl, ed., *The Question Book* (Nashville: Thomas Nelson, 1993), p. ix.
3. See, for example, the chapter "Cultivate Koinonia."
4. D. Martyn Lloyd-Jones, *Spiritual Depression: Its Causes and Cure* (Grand Rapids, Mich.: Eerdmans, 1965), p. 224.
5. Wayne A. Detzler, *New Testament Words in Today's Language* (Colorado Springs, Colo.: Cook Communications, 1986), p. 396.
6. John Owen, *An Exposition of the Epistle to the Hebrews,* vol. 7, W. H. Goold, ed. (1855; reprint, Grand Rapids, Mich.: Baker, 1980), p. 425.

7. Owen, p. 421.
8. C. H. Spurgeon, *Lectures to My Students*, four volumes in one (London: Passmore and Alabaster, 1881-94; reprint ed., Pasadena, Tex.: Pilgrim Publications, 1990), 2:65–68.
9. Richard Baxter, *The Autobiography of Richard Baxter*, abridged by J. M. Lloyd Thomas, ed., and with an introductions by N. H. Keeble (introduction and notes, London: J. M. Dent & Sons, 1931; reprint with revisions, Totowa, N.J.: Rowman and Littlefield, 1974), p. 94.
10. Baxter, p. 94.

Simplifying and Your Heart

1. Iain H. Murray, D. Martyn Lloyd-Jones: *The First Forty Years 1899-1939* (Edinburgh: The Banner of Truth Trust, 1982), p. 98.

Simplifying and Your Time

1. The Editors of Country Beautiful, *A Man of Destiny: Winston S. Churchill* (Waukesha, Wis.: Country Beautiful Foundation, 1965), pp. 66-67.
2. Richard A. Swenson, *More Than Meets the Eye* (Colorado Springs, Colo.: NavPress, 2000), p. 55.
3. John Piper, *A Godward Life* (Sisters, Ore.: Multnomah, 1999), p. 364.
4. If you do, see "Why Go to Church?" in Donald S. Whitney, *Spiritual Disciplines Within the Church* (Chicago: Moody, 1996), pp. 15-30.
5. Bruce Horovitz, "24/7 almost a way of life," *USA Today,* 1 August 2001, p. 1.

Simplifying and Others

1. London Confession of Faith (Baptist), 22.6; Westminster Confession of Faith (Presbyterian), 21.6.
2. Wayne Martindale and Jerry Root, eds., *The Quotable Lewis* (Wheaton, Ill.: Tyndale, 1989), p. 90.
3. As quoted in John Blanchard, comp., *More Gathered Gold* (Welwyn, Hertfordshire, England: Evangelical Press, 1986), p. 291.
4. Eugene H. Peterson, *Subversive Spirituality* (Grand Rapids, Mich.: Eerdmans, 1997), p. 178.
5. As quoted in *Current Thoughts and Trends,* August 2000, p. 17.

ABOUT THE AUTHOR

DONALD S. WHITNEY is an associate professor of biblical spirituality at the Southern Baptist Theological Seminary in Louisville, Kentucky, and is currently completing a Th.D. at the University of South Africa. He is the author of *Spiritual Disciplines for the Christian Life*, *Ten Questions to Diagnose Your Spiritual Health*, and *How Can I Be Sure I'm a Christian?* (all NavPress). Don holds a doctor of ministry degree from Trinity Evangelical Divinity School in Deerfield, Illinois, and was previously a professor of Spiritual Formation at Midwestern Baptist Theological Seminary in Kansas City, Missouri, for ten years. Don's wife, Caffy, ministers from their home as a women's Bible study teacher, an artist, and a freelance illustrator. The Whitneys are parents of a daughter, Laurelen Christiana. You may subscribe to Don's free e-mail newsletter at his website, www.BiblicalSpirituality.org.